To Nikita —
May you always be
" Dipped In It "

WORLDCHANGERS
M E D I A

bethany harvey

DIPPED
IN IT

a memoir

PAPERBACK: 978-0-9993991-4-9
E-BOOK: 978-0-9993991-5-6

FIRST PAPERBACK EDITION: July 2021
Library of Congress Control Number: 2021909714

EDITED BY Bryna Haynes / www.The AuthorRevolution.com
COVER ART by Beau Harvey /
LAYOUT BY Ivica Jandrijevic / www.WritingNights.org

LINE ART CREDITS FOR DIPPED IN IT
p27, 33, @ Simple Line via AdobeStock; p41, 243, 290, 334 @Valenty via AdobeStock; p44, 260 @Nataletado via DepositPhotos; p69 @OneLineStock.com via AdobeStock; p91 @Mihail via AdobeStock; p107 @ JustArtNina via ShutterStock; p108 @OneLineStock.com via ShutterStock; p187 @Valenty via ShutterStock; p149 @ vgorbash via AdobeStock; p195 @Keya via AdobeStock; p200 @LivDeco via ShutterStock; p277 @IhorZigor via ShutterStock; p295 @Singleline via ShutterStock

PUBLISHED BY WorldChangers Media
PO Box 83, Foster, RI 02825
www.WorldChangers.Media

DEDICATION

*To Ruby and Beau: may you always know
that you are "dipped in it."*

PEOPLE ARE SAYING ...

"Bethany has an uncanny way of speaking directly to the heart about what it means to be on this messy human journey. Thoughtful, impactful, and deeply transformative, her stories, insights, heartbreaks, and humor make us more open to being 'tenderized' by our experiences, as well as incredibly grateful to share the same planet as such an intelligent, witty, and wise human being. She writes with a grace that stays with you long after you turn the final page. This book is a revelation."

—Monica Rodgers, founder, The Revelation Project

"I could not stop reading the tender, openhearted, and gentle reflections that Bethany shares about her life after the death of her father. I was so moved by her graceful ability to notice, process, and move forward from experiences that shape us all. You will be glued to every page as you eagerly wait for the next bit of juicy wisdom to subtly fall in your lap."

—Kim Fuller, Author of *Finding*, founder of Born to Rise

"Bethany Harvey's *Dipped In It* is poetic and wise. Her stories grab you with their simple truth and shine light on the cold fact that love—and all the glory that comes with it—is inextricably bound to loss and grief. She manages to do this in a way that knocks the breath out of your chest, yet somehow you're not sorry, or even sad. Instead, you're elated by the privilege of getting to experience this raw, tender paradox of being human."

—Sarah MacLaughlin, author of the award-winning, bestselling book, *What Not to Say, Tools for Talking with Young Children* and the forthcoming, *Raising Humans with Heart: Not a How-To Manual*

"Bethany's deftly-crafted storytelling connected effortlessly with my consciousness as it gently reached down and knocked on the door of my heart. She yanked my own buried emotions up to the surface to be revealed as she gently cradled my forgotten feelings in the beauty of her compassionate prose, reminding me that the truth is the only way to real freedom."

— **Carrie Rowan, bestselling author of** *Tell A New Story*,
coach, and award-winning singer/songwriter

"An easy and delicious read! *Dipped in It* effortlessly combines storytelling and self-care so the reader walks away with many 'a-ha' moments. Bethany has gifted the reader with insight into her own life, helping us find the joy, compassion, and funny moments in our own journeys."

—**Jennifer Neuguth, founder and CEO of Iamtra**

"What stands out most about *Dipped in It*, what makes it so deeply special, is that it speaks to everyone. No, we haven't shared the same life experiences. But we've all—every one of us—shared the feelings unique to them. The threads of those shared emotions bind us to one another, and Bethany, through her writing, is the weaver of them, carefully, lovingly cinching us together into a tapestry where we can look to our right and our left and see that we're not alone. Love connects us. Bethany is a gift, and we're all her lucky recipients."

—**Kim Beauchamp, ND Author/Activist Making DIPG History**

"Bethany tackles the messiness of life and loss with grace, honesty, and humor. From the first word, her raw, open writing style pulled me in. I laughed with her, cried with her, and cheered her on every step of the way. Grab a box of tissues, pour a cup of tea, and enjoy!"

—**Tabitha Lord, award-winning author of the** *HORIZON* **series**

"*Dipped In It* is a beautiful meditation on one's hopes and dreams, on gratitude through life's highs and lows, and on the power of grief. Bethany Harvey's exquisite writing pulls you through the pages and her reflections on her life will give you insight into your own. A thoroughly enjoyable memoir!"

— **Judy Crosby, owner/founder, Island Books**

TABLE OF CONTENTS

INTRODUCTION

Have you ever been going along in life, thinking everything is unfolding exactly as it should, and then ... you fall deep, deep into a well of grief, sadness, and uncertainty?

In January of 2017, my father passed away. And I was tossed into the deepest, darkest well I'd ever seen or envisioned—without warning or ceremony.

There I was, in the dark. And something inside of me said, quietly, *"The only way out is to write."*

I started with a gratitude journal. I needed to remind myself of all of the people in my life for whom I ought to be grateful. I write "ought to" because at the time I believed that I wasn't a grateful person. Not anymore. Grateful people don't feel the way I felt—angry, anxious, depressed, confused, disillusioned, desperate (to name a few of grief's cohorts).

Looking back, I realize that what I was actually trying to do with this gratitude journal was *avoid* my grief. *Ah, a loophole! If I can just be grateful, I won't have to grieve anymore—because one cannot do both, obviously.*

I didn't know that gratitude and grief are *not* mutually exclusive. But I learned. I learned I couldn't skip over the emotions that made me uncomfortable. And in the end, I didn't want to. There is a complicated brew of emotions swirling inside each of us.

It's what makes us feel alive.

And so, with trembling hands upon my keyboard, I offered myself this saving grace—permission to indulge them all, the whole wild cup of tea.

And now, here you are, holding in your hands, the liquid grace of grief, joy, gratitude, fear, sadness, anger, and most of all, *love*. The juice of life that filled my well high enough that I could reach for the top and finally climb out, back into the tremulous sunshine of daily living.

Dip your cup, dear reader. It may taste familiar.

Dipped In It

My dad used to say if someone was particularly lucky or blessed, they were "dipped in it." If I pulled out some unexpected victory, he'd shake his head with a grin, and emphasize each word as he said, "Bethany Anne, you are Dipped. In. It." Dipped in what, specifically? I had no idea, but in these moments, I felt golden.

Though one of the humblest men I've ever known, my father always knew he was dipped in it. He would say it about me often, too, and I believed him. I was.

But am I still?

As morning creeps in, I lie here thinking about the past few years of my life. I realize that this breaking open I am experiencing has been building for years. My father's death was the final blow. I know finding myself here in pieces is an entirely *human* experience. It is also an entirely uncomfortable one. I am exhausted. Steeped in sadness. I am often lonely even while surrounded by love.

How do people *do* this? How do they feel *all of this* and survive? I long to find my way back to the person I was before the cracks began to form. I wonder if I could even relate to her anymore. Memory paints her light as a feather—and here I am, dragging around my anvil collection.

I will my legs over the side of the bed, toes searching for the well-worn, cozy shearling of my father's slippers. I look down at this priceless inheritance—coffee stained, with an errant thread threatening to disembowel one slipper with a mere tug. I shoved them into my overnight bag the morning after the funeral, obscuring them beneath a sea of black, as if I would be searched on the way out. As if I'd be caught and shamed for attempting to abscond with a precious family heirloom. In the end I confessed that I was taking them, feeling a pang of guilt that this revelation came as a statement and not a question. I worried for a moment that my mother would try to pass off to me instead, the pristine pair he'd been given days ago for Christmas. I suspect she looked at me and understood that those would never do. Because *these* slippers—these warm and messy and perfect slippers—were what I needed to arm myself with that morning, as I walked out of his house and into a world that was shamelessly carrying on without him.

Two months have passed since that day, and putting my feet into these slippers each morning has become a necessary ritual for me. I am sure he would make a joke about me "walking in his shoes." It's really more of a shuffle because they are way too big. That would be funny to him, too. His shoes are literally too big for me to fill.

I try.

L'Irony

Months ago, before Dad passed away and our whole world changed, I bought four tickets to bring my daughters and my mother to the theater to see *The Lion King*.

I am not known for my organizational skills, nor for my tech savvy. And so it happened that it wasn't until the morning of the show that I remembered I would soon need the e-tickets that had been emailed to me six months prior. Perhaps you would have printed them out right away, or taken a screen shot, or bookmarked them, but I am afraid this is not me, even in the best of times.

Opening my laptop, I found that for some reason I could not retrieve any emails. The e-tickets were lost somewhere in cyberspace. My stomach lurched.

It seemed desperately important that we go to this show. I needed to prove to all of us that we could enjoy something we had planned to do before we were robbed of Dad. *Life goes on, you see! We can still do all the things!*

I knew the best person to help me find the e-tickets was my friend, Austin. I texted him, with the sort of pleading you can imagine a woman might employ when she is desperately trying to orchestrate access to a show that starts in two hours, for a mother who has barely set foot outside her home in two months.

But pleading is never necessary with Austin. True to form, he showed up five minutes later. Not a call—he just showed up. Austin always shows up, eager to help me or my kids in any way possible. *Let me take care of that for you* is his perpetual gesture.

And so, we were saved!

Sort of.

It was only after we settled into the plush velvet seats of the theater and the house lights fell, that I remembered the *plot* of *The Lion King*.

The father dies.

Snakeskin

Alone for the first time in weeks, I have had a very bizarre weekend. I have experienced huge fluctuations in emotion—from giddily dancing around in my underwear to Stevie Wonder to bawling my eyes out on my couch.

When I feel truly happy these days, it is such an unexpected emotion that I feel a euphoric rush (cue Stevie Wonder). When I actually allow myself to sit in the anger and sadness, it feels paralyzing.

Holy mood swings.

I messaged my friend, Monica, and asked her if she thought it was possible that I am actually bipolar. She responded that I am the *least* bipolar person she knows. (That sounds really funny in hindsight, as if she had previously conducted an assessment of the bipolarishness of all her acquaintances).

She may be right. I tend to be even-keeled to the extreme. I once had a friend spend the better part of an evening trying to force me to "get angry!" (I never did.) When it comes to anger, I tend to be measured. I consider what my role is in the situation. I consider what might have led the other person to behave the way they did. I consider whether there is any point in engaging. (I usually decide there isn't.)

I shed tears with frequency but it's not often that I allow myself the release of a deep, primal cry. Cathartic as I know it may be, the complete release of control in that way is entirely unappealing. I am open, generous, and eager when it comes to expressing love and affection, joy and laughter ... but sadness and anger? No, thank you.

I will resist, avoid and shove down those emotions for as long as I possibly can. I am finally realizing that this may be a problem. Because despite my controlled outward response, I still feel. Deeply. My skin hasn't actually gotten any thicker ... and I'm growing less and less comfortable living in it.

I recently made an analogy to my friend, Michael, about wanting to shed my skin like a snake. I want to peel away everything that is making me feel uncomfortable in my body—the anger, the sadness, the loneliness. He replied that perhaps it is time to do just that.

And while what I really want is just to get rid of it, this uncomfortable skin—to unzip it and step out, unscathed—I have come to realize that the snake does not just shimmy out of her skin. She does not simply slip it off. She rubs herself against rough surfaces in order to release this sheathing that once protected her but no longer fits. It is uncomfortable. Instinctively, she knows there is no other way to be free.

It's Not Pie

There is a quote that has been circulating lately online: *"Equal rights for others does not mean fewer rights for you. It's not pie."*

I have been thinking about how this applies to compassion. I used to imagine that if I expressed how I was really feeling, people would think, "Why does she think her pain is so much bigger than everyone else's? Doesn't she know that I'm suffering too? Can't she see that so-and-so has it so much worse than she does?"

I now recognize this largely as projection on my part—that I felt uncomfortable fully owning and expressing my own grief, because I was (and am) fully aware that there are *so many* people suffering greater tragedies than I.

Yet to me, my own grief is enormous. I'm learning that I am allowed to feel this grief fully. That this is okay. That feeling my own pain deeply does not make me blind and deaf to the suffering of others. In fact, I am learning that fully standing in my own feelings can open up a reserve of compassion like nothing else—because pain recognizes pain.

Just as love can be infinite, so can compassion. Offering myself a big serving of self- compassion does not mean I have less to offer to others.

It's not pie.

Peeling the Onion
(Part One)

Four and half years ago, my husband, who I'll call Charlie, and I headed into what would be the last couple's counseling session of our marriage.

I did not know this at that time. I thought Charlie had agreed to give counseling another try because he was still trying to save our marriage. That he was, like me, throwing up one last Hail Mary.

It occurred to me much later that he agreed to go because he wanted the support of the counselor—for both of us—when he told me what he needed to share. This was smart. Because honestly, had we not been there, in so official a setting, I may not have taken him seriously. How can a woman take it seriously when the man with whom she's been in an intimate relationship for the past twelve years—with whom she has two very traditionally produced daughters—tells her he is gay?

But the fact of the matter is this: whether it made sense to me or not was entirely inconsequential. The much more relevant point, of which I grabbed ahold with the raw desperation of a drowning woman, was this: I was free.

I was free—and it wasn't my fault.

I hadn't failed. There was a reason, an excuse—a get out of jail free card. When he turned to me as we sat side by side on that virtual stranger's couch, and said the words, "I'm gay," I remember the room spinning for a minute, as if I might faint. And then I heard the words pour from my mouth, as if riding out of my body upon the wave of relief that coursed through me.

"I guess we're getting a divorce," I said.

Thank God, I thought.

Even now, writing this, I feel as though I should be ashamed of that—of my eagerness to abandon my marriage. I was raised to believe that divorce is wrong. Not in a "It's a sin against God" kind of way, but in a "You made a commitment, and you are a person of integrity" kind of way.

A couple of months earlier, I had finally gathered the courage to tell my parents that divorce seemed imminent. This was a surprise to them, as I had kept my cards close to my chest on the matter of our unhappiness. I had never wanted to admit our failure. Not until I couldn't bear to live that way anymore—pretending to be the perfect family.

When I told them, my father looked so disappointed. "Please give it one more try," he said. And so I did.

Of course, I knew he would love me anyway. He would embrace the new normal. He would be supportive. But that *look*. I never wanted him to look at me like that again. Disappointment was not an expression I was used to seeing on my father's face—especially not when it was directed at me.

Revisiting the conversation months later (and now armed with this ironclad excuse), I had the courage to tell my parents emphatically, "I am getting a divorce ..." (again, the dreaded look—but, oh, Dad, *wait for it*) "... because Charlie is gay."

It was a completely perverse triumph. There it was, the raw truth: I'd rather have a gay husband than a disappointed father.

My mother later told me that the next morning my father woke up, rolled over to face her, and said wryly, "I had the *strangest* dream about Bethany."

So, what does one do next, you wonder? Well, in my very limited experience, one gets entirely schnockered. My brothers, sisters-in-law, and cousins took me out for what continues to rank up there as one of the most fun nights of my life. We all got rip-roaring drunk, laughed a lot … and then went dancing. Well, to be accurate, the women went dancing while the men stood at a safe distance so as not to be associated with us. I cannot remember the last time I had so much fun.

That is, until the next morning, when the reality of my life came surging up from my belly straight into the toilet.

The weeks that followed were some of the most tender in our entire married life. I know this may be hard to believe. I think it's because it was such a relief to have made a decision after being unhappy for so long. We were able to love and appreciate each other again—perhaps with a bit of nostalgia for who we once were to each other, and tenderness for who we hoped we'd always be.

But it wasn't all relief and optimism. There was our mutual devastation over what we were about to do to our children. We had no illusions about that. They were so little. When we sat down to tell them we would be living in separate houses, what they heard was that *we* would now have *two* houses. They were delighted.

And so, for those final weeks of cohabitation, we savored our family time, bittersweet as it was. He and I slept in the same bed, taking turns being the one sobbing quietly in the dark—so the girls wouldn't hear—while the other clung closely, offering comfort. Knowing there was no place for us to go but forward.

Armpit Heart

My daughter, Ruby, handed me a warm, soft, beautiful heart, made of beeswax.

"This is for you!" she beamed.

"Oh, that's so sweet," I said, "Thank you!"

"I warmed it up in my armpit!" she exclaimed.

"Oh, um ... lovely?" I smirked.

We giggled, but I was thinking (stay with me, because who doesn't love metaphors about armpits?) ... is the beeswax heart a less tender offering because of where it has been? Can we assume that *every* heart has been through something? What if we are open and honest about what our hearts have endured? What if we speak of them in clear, unwavering voices? What if we take the risk to say, *"Here is my heart. Let me tell you of the dark places it has been ...*

"Do you still think it's beautiful?

"Will you keep it?"

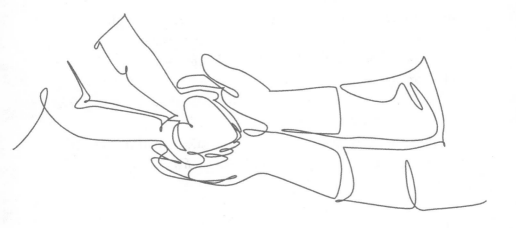

Nourishment

Between his heart attack and his passing, my father was in a coma for ten days. During that time, I would sit with him for long periods, often overnight. I had very little thought of food, and would come home periodically only to shower and to nap. Sometimes I would come home to find that friends had left me soup, a casserole, cookies, fruit, energy bars, or my favorite coffee.

There may be no gesture more beautiful than to say, *I know you are too overwhelmed to take care of yourself right now, so we are going to help you. We want to nourish you.*

I was so grateful.

After the funeral, life went on around us. I went back to work and I resumed my usual life patterns and responsibilities, even though doing so felt disrespectful in some way, even perverse. How could we all just proceed as if the world had not been irreparably changed?

Somehow, I felt as though I was supposed to bounce right back. Suck it up, warrior on. During this time, it felt strange to accept offers of meals. I'll even go so far as to say I felt ashamed, worried that it meant people thought me weak, or incapable.

I was not those things. What I was, though, was exhausted. And sad. And preoccupied by worry over the emotional well-being of my family. Yet, my pride wanted me to say to these gracious offers of food, "No thank you. I've got it handled."

Then, someone near and dear to me said something very important. She said, "Just shut up and *take the food!*"

She was right, of course. People wanted to do something, and this was about the only thing they could think of to do. It was needed. And it was so lovely.

The beautiful thing about meals that come from a place of love and compassion is that they nourish more than the body. They nourish the heart, and the soul, too. So, I encourage you that if you find yourself in a place in which you are utterly exhausted by life, and somebody offers to nourish you—body, heart, and soul—*please* just say, "Thank you."

Then, shut up and take the food.

Two Shits

I have always thought of myself as a lucky person. Maybe it had to do with, as my Uncle Ed would say, "being born in the right cradle."

I was not spoiled with material things growing up, but I never wanted for much. My parents paid in full for my four-year degree, a privilege I didn't fully appreciate until years later when I noticed friends struggling with school loans.

I took the first job I was offered after college, an entry-level gig I thought would be a summer job. Five years later I was given the opportunity to run that business (a private preschool). When Charlie and I had our first child, and then our second, I wanted to stay at home, and I did. Five years later, just weeks after learning we could no longer afford for me to continue to do so, the opportunity to open my own preschool seemed to fall into my lap. Beau went off to kindergarten and Ruby came to work with me. The timing and the nature of my work made perfect what I thought would be a sad transition.

I felt "dipped in it," even in crisis. When Charlie and I had our moment at the therapist's office, I immediately saw the silver lining. The dissolution of our marriage set me free. When divorce became a reality, I knew I did not want to stay in our family home. I needed to escape, to be the one to inhabit a new space—but as a new business owner, there was not much money.

I called a few realtors who were not optimistic about matching my income with anything inspiring—and the idea of moving my kids into a gloomy place felt awful. Then, I looked on Craigslist.

The very first listing that popped up was a very beautiful (and very tiny) guesthouse on a farm—a dreamy little haven nestled under hundred-year-old beech trees. Even better, it was within my budget. The property owners were wonderful and embraced the girls and me like family. I knew this home would be healing for all of us.

It was easy to believe in silver linings—in things "happening for a reason"—when I always managed to land on my feet. At times throughout my life, I've worried that things for me have been just too easy—that life could not possibly continue to go so smoothly.

In a way, I was right. But not in the way I expected.

When my father died, I bottomed out. I lost faith. I cannot imagine a reason, nor a silver lining, in his death. It just feels cruel.

My grandmother once said to me, "Bethany, nobody likes to be shat upon." I marveled at—and was highly amused by—her ability to express this sentiment in an eloquent and dignified manner.

Right now, in the wake of Dad's death, I feel shat upon by the Universe.

As they do, children tend to give us reminders about the beauty of having a positive outlook. Ruby said to me recently, "Mom! Did you know that it is actually *lucky* when a bird poops on you?!"

"Is that so?" I replied, amused.

"Yes!" she exclaimed, "and I've already been lucky twice and I'm only seven!"

Ah, perspective. I'll get there.

Birthday Candle
Sunrise

Today is Ruby's eighth birthday. Last night, when I was snuggling her into bed, I said, "This is the last time I will see you as a seven-year-old. Do you think you will still want to snuggle me when you're eight?"

"Yes," she said, thoughtfully. "I think I'll snuggle you until I'm sixteen. After that I'll be busy driving around with my friends."

(I have no doubt she's right.)

In the middle of the night, she crawled in with me. So, for the start of her eighth year, we woke up together, cozy in my bed. Outside my bedroom window the sky was ablaze with the most vibrant sunrise I have ever seen. It was completely stunning. It felt as though this show of Mother Nature's was entirely for us. She had lit Ruby's birthday candles all across the horizon.

I have a friend who says she can see and hear angels. I believe her because she just … *knows things*. She has always said that Ruby is surrounded by angels wherever she goes. I believe that, too. There's just something about her that is magical, otherworldly.

She's the child who senses when I could use a little tender loving care and wordlessly brings me a cup of tea, quietly curling up nearby—offering the warmth that her proximity provides. I often joke that she will be the one to take care of me when I'm old (well … I say I'm joking, but really I'm not). She is a natural nurturer. She seems intuitively connected with the emotions of those around her. She feels her own storms deeply but allows them to pass quickly through her. And she is often the one to sit calmly with others while they experience their own passing storms.

One sleepy evening Ruby said to me, "Mama, you make *everything* better."

I thought my heart would burst.

It is actually Ruby who makes everything better. I am just grateful to have been invited along for the ride.

Imagination

"The bravest person in the world must not have a very good imagination," says my ten-year-old daughter, Beau, as we lay in bed together.

"Hmm, what do you mean by that?" I ask, intrigued.

"Well, they are probably so brave because they can't *imagine* anything bad ever happening. They don't even know what to be afraid of."

Considering this, I ask, "So, would you rather be the bravest person, or the one with the best imagination?"

Without hesitation (and perhaps with just a hint of surprise) she replies, "The best imagination! If you can't imagine the bad stuff, you can't imagine the good stuff either! You'd never know what to hope for. You'd never be proud of yourself, because you could never imagine that you might have failed or might have been scared. You'd never learn anything, because you could never imagine there was anything else to know. Life would be very boring."

Then she kisses my forehead and rolls over to go to sleep.

I lay there, stunned, willing myself to remember every word of what she'd just said, because it was the most profound thing I'd heard in a long time.

It is conversations like this one that leave me with little doubt that Beau will ultimately teach me *way* more about how to live a rich life than I could ever teach her. She is an impassioned poet, a writer of love songs. She is a bedtime philosopher, and a giver of infinite hugs. She is a girl of powerful resolve, a fiery fighter of injustices—real *and* imagined. She is the safe harbor and the tempest, both. She is one of the most intuitive, profound, and complex people I know … and she has only just begun.

And I Love You

My brothers and I stood side by side in the receiving line at Dad's wake. Dad's elderly aunt, who is beginning to experience dementia, was going through the line. She stopped in front of me. Remembering my face, but not my name, she smiled and hugged me. Ryan was next, and not recognizing him (though she's known him well his whole life) she introduced herself. Ryan, ever full of compassion and warmth said, "Yes, I know who you are. I'm Bill's son, Ryan ... and I love you."

She smiled broadly, and he gave her a warm hug.

The next day we stood together on the altar, my brothers and I, giving our father's eulogy in tandem. Ryan had doubts that he would be able to do this—that he could get up and speak about our dad without falling apart.

He spoke about our dad's strong character, his integrity and lack of ego, his loyalty and kindness. Ryan said, "To be the man that my father was would be a difficult task. But, if we always remember his principles, and strive to live our lives as he did, I truly believe our lives will be as full of happiness and love as the life my father lived."

What I find so beautiful about Ryan and his aspirations to be like my dad is this: he doesn't know that he already is.

Brave Face

A few weeks ago, my girls and I were visiting a friend. She and I talked quietly about how I was coping with my father's death, while the girls colored nearby. Beau drew a portrait of a woman, her face split in two. One side was smiling, with golden hair and bright colors. She wore a crown of flowers. The other side of her face was bathed in blues and purples. She wore a frown and a crown of thorns. When I looked at it, I saw myself. *Is this the person she has been living with for the last three months?*

Then, last week, I heard from an old friend who shared that her biggest regret as a parent is that she never showed her children how to be vulnerable. She thought she'd been protecting them by always showing them a strong façade and hiding her pain, particularly throughout her divorce. In hindsight she thought, "How can a child learn that it's okay to feel deeply if they've never seen that modeled for them?"

I haven't really talked about grief much with my kids. They may see me cloud up or tear up, but I usually hold it back, push it down. I wait to cry until I'm in the shower or alone in my car. As parents we want to protect our children from—well, from *everything*. Even from feelings.

But I am not fooling my children by pushing back tears and putting on a "brave face" (whatever that means).

Please don't misunderstand me: as parents, perhaps our most important job is to reassure our children that their foundation is solid. They need to feel safe. We can't be a hot mess all the time. However,

I understand now that it is okay for my children to see the tears flow. More importantly, it's okay to talk to them about how I am feeling.

Our children already know when we are sad. We don't want them to learn sadness is something they should feel ashamed of—something that should be pushed down and buttoned up. We should not shelter them from seeing us feel, from seeing us grieve. What a gift to allow them to see that true healing takes time and self-compassion, and that it involves a whole spectrum of emotions that are *all* worthy and important.

Risk

I have had quite a bit of experience with the unexpected. Not situations where I took risks that didn't pan out, but rather situations in which I had become comfortable with the seeming stability and predictability of things and was then unceremoniously reminded that there is no such thing.

I can understand why it has become instinctual to cling not only to my loved ones, but also to patterns of behavior—habits that provide the illusion of predictability and control. Taking risks, in life and in love, seems entirely foolhardy. After all, it's scary enough that I have so little control. Why would I willingly invite havoc or heartbreak?

Living with two mystical creatures such as I do, I often find "potions" around my house in recycled jars and paint containers. A black, murky liquid might be marked *Deadly Nightshade* or *Witches' Brew*. I recently came across one labeled *Risk*. It was a tiny, fairy-sized bottle filled with golden glitter. It struck me that rather than it being a dark and foreboding concoction, *Risk* was instead luminous and magical, golden and glittery. I realized that, to my children, risk is a thrilling exploration of what is possible.

I wondered: if I can admit to myself that I control nothing, is it possible to find a place of freedom, rather than fear, in the not knowing? Can I once again begin to see *risk* as something *beautiful?*

Perspective

I snapped a photo during an early morning walk this week. I love how it plays with perspective—one can see the Newport Bridge on the horizon, which from a distance looks quite small, while the dock in the foreground looks enormous in comparison. A silhouette of a seagull against the sun also plays with size and distance.

This image made me think about how we relate to things in our daily lives. Small things, or small problems, often seem enormous when they are directly in front of us. Sometimes they are all we can see, obscuring our view of anything else—especially when we choose to focus on them.

But when we are able to step back and consider the big picture, we are able to put things into perspective. By taking this wider view, we can see that the problem is relatively small. This, of course, helps to calm us, and allows us to handle the issue in a healthier way.

It is much more difficult to shift our perspective when it comes to big life traumas. For one thing—they actually are big, and we know it. They are hard to minimize, and that is okay. We are entitled to feel their enormity.

It seems to me that sometimes the only way to change our relationship to these big traumas is to allow for the distance that can be gained only through time. We will always know, within, that the size of it has not changed, just as the size of the bridge does not actually change as we move away from it. But hopefully, in time, we will find ourselves far enough away that our traumas will cease to obscure—or even throw shadows across—our world view.

We're All Mad Here, Alice

Well, hello, Anxiety! I should've known you'd show up. It's because of what I wrote about risk, isn't it? Because I suggested we shouldn't worry, because nothing is really within our control anyway? I thought so.

Anxiety has arrived to call bullshit on my new, fun-loving, bohemian view on risk—on seeing the unknown as beautiful. And it has landed powerfully.

Oh, and I see you've brought your friend, Fear. How lovely! Please, make yourselves at home.

This morning I was entirely (and *completely* irrationally) convinced that some terrible fate had befallen my friend, Michael—a friend with whom I happen to be entirely (and, it seems, hopelessly) in love. Two romantic stops and starts between us have left me somewhat inexplicably enraptured.

Part of me knew I was being irrational with my fear of his untimely demise. (Fortunately, that was the part of me that willed myself to wait ten minutes for his text response before going off in search of his lifeless body). The other, very visceral part of me had already lodged my racing heart *well* up into my throat.

The thing is, you can talk about risk and lack of predictability, and about releasing the illusion of control, but if you are a parent, a child, a sister or brother, a husband or wife, a lover, or a devoted friend ...

Let me simplify. *Do you love? Are you loved?* Then I don't believe you can ever be truly free from the fear of loss—especially when you have lost before.

I also know that we can't allow Anxiety and Fear to own us, or put us into a panic when someone we love goes out of view or isn't where they are meant to be (small children aside). I know I will have to learn to relax my grip on the steering wheel of life. I already know I'm not driving.

When I heard from Michael (who was entirely *not* dead), and I told him how insane I felt, he replied, with a smile in his voice, "We're all mad here, Alice."

Indeed, as C.S. Lewis wrote: "*You must be mad, or you wouldn't have come.*"

Misplaced Purse

Sometimes I have these moments of panic that I am going to lose my memories of my dad. I frantically search my mind the way a nervous woman might plunge her hand into her misplaced purse. As her fingers grasp each familiar item—her wallet, her phone, her keys (his laugh, his smile, his humor)—she slowly begins to relax.

Breathe. It's all still in here.

Holding Their Gaze

My brother, Bill, is a funny guy. He is often sarcastic, with a quick wit and a gift for one-liners. While there is no doubt he loves his family and friends, I never would describe Bill as particularly affectionate, nor emotive. But Bill was hit hard by our father's death. He saw Dad every day; he shared an office with him, just as Dad had shared an office with his father before him.

Over these last few months, I have come to the surprising realization that Bill may be the most sensitive of us all. There is something about experiencing a great loss that cracks a person open, revealing parts of them that had been previously hidden. I see now that, hidden beneath Bill's intensity and sarcasm, is truly the most tender heart.

When you look into a person's eyes and see your own pain reflected back at you, you have two choices. You can decide it's too painful to look there. You can stop meeting their gaze, and your relationship will begin to wither. Or, you can hold their gaze, and truly see each other in all of your brokenness.

My brothers and I have chosen to hold each other's gaze. I believe we see each other now in a way we never have before. There was always love, but now I feel devotion between us that is deeper and more authentic than I could have imagined. Had we not been so mutually wrecked by this loss, perhaps we would never have known how truly, and how deeply, we love one another.

Pictures of Me

My mother has always been a beautiful woman. A petite blond with large, hazel eyes, she looks a decade younger than her age suggests she should. Mom is an avid and talented photographer. She has a gift for capturing the warmth and emotion of a moment in time, allowing us all to hold these moments in our hands and close to our hearts, timelessly.

Over the years, my mom took many beautiful photos of my dad, especially of him enjoying his family. Looking through all of these photos after Dad died, it became alarming to me how few photos there are of her. She is always behind the camera. This suddenly seemed a glaring omission.

I told her, "We need to take more photos of you from now on."

She looked at me and said, quite matter-of-factly, "When I die, the photos that you will have—*of me*—will be the photos I have taken all of my life of everything and everyone that I love."

Death's Dichotomy

Yesterday was Easter, and our first holiday without my dad. While none of us are particularly religious, it was a day we would have all been together.

In the early morning I donned Dad's baseball hat and ventured out into our "church." It was a glorious morning in the woods. I found myself feeling him with me so palpably—and, at the same time, missing him so much that I ached.

I got to thinking about this brutal and beautiful paradox: he is both nowhere and everywhere, all at once.

He is with my mom as she pours her coffee and watches the birds from her kitchen window. He is with his grandchildren as they tear into their chocolate rabbits. He is here with me in the woods, and he will be with us as we toast him at dinner.

We are left to painfully miss someone who never actually leaves us. He is everywhere.

Peeling the Onion
(Part Two)

In many ways, I liked the idea of Charlie being gay. It was convenient. It made our divorce clean, in a "throw your hands in the air and declare there's nothing more to be done" kind of way. In fact, when I told a friend what was happening, she joked, "I'm seventy-five percent sure I wish *my* husband were gay."

I secretly loved the idea that Charlie would, from that point forward, never have another relationship with a woman. There would be no other woman of whom to feel jealous. There would be no other woman trying to mother my daughters.

And then, ten months after I moved out, a woman moved into Charlie's house. She was (or would soon become) Charlie's girlfriend. The jig was up.

While I never felt foolish for people believing I had married a gay man, it was quite humbling having people deduce that my husband lied about being gay in order to get rid of me. Or that I had lied about him being gay in order to get rid of him.

As it often does, the truth lay somewhere in the middle. I never questioned whether Charlie was gay, because it was easier for me not to. And I suspect that Charlie was just trying to ease us all toward her truth in the gentlest way she knew how.

You see, Charlie is not, as it turns out, a gay man. She is actually a gay woman.

Charlie is transgender.

And so, the irony came to light that the "other woman" who would be mothering my children would, in fact, be Charlie.

There was always something feminine about Charlie. To be honest, I always loved that about her. I don't tend to go for partners who are dripping with testosterone. I like a man with a softness about him. Should I have been tipped off that there was more to it for Charlie than being comfortable with her feminine side? Perhaps. When she pirouetted from the stove to the refrigerator to grab the butter, should I have questioned her masculinity? Maybe. But even if I had deemed this behavior "unmanly," rather than quirky and endearing, believe me when I tell you that I never could have imagined that the first transgender person I would meet would be my husband.

Still, as foreign a concept as this was for me at the time, it made sense. In fact, somehow, this revelation made *much* more sense to me than Charlie being gay.

Unfortunately, Charlie's feminine energy never manifested itself in the desire or ability to share her deepest thoughts and feelings. Once, while we lay in bed together, each glued to our own screen, she sent me an email accusing me of (calling me out on? Because she wasn't wrong!) carrying on an emotional affair, via messaging, with an old boyfriend. She composed it, sent it, and then lay there watching me as I read it—all in complete silence.

It is not hard to understand why Charlie never developed the skill of being vulnerable. When you have spent decades of your life with a deep-seated fear that the truth of who you are won't be accepted, I imagine you learn to put up a lot of walls to protect yourself. Revealing bits of her authentic self must have been terrifying for Charlie—like voluntarily shooting cannons at the very walls that kept her safe.

And so, in typical Charlie fashion, rather than to speak with me in person about this small matter of her gender identity, she chose to inform me via text. At 10:30 p.m. on a Saturday night, two and half years after we'd split, she sent me a photo of herself standing on the sidewalk in our old neighborhood wearing a dress, makeup, and a wig.

For a moment, I thought I was looking at a photo of her sister. And then I saw. I saw *her.*

Can you stand it? she wrote. *Oh my God! Don't show anyone.*

Stunned, I shifted my body to shield the screen from my date. I had just explained apologetically to the man sitting beside me on my couch that I had to read the text from my ex-husband when it came through. Charlie and I had an agreement that we would not text each other after 9:00 p.m. unless it was an emergency. (I had no idea "emergency" was about to be redefined for me).

"Okay," I wrote, somewhat numbly, as confusion and panic seemed to drain the blood from my body. I tried to make sense of what I was seeing—was it a Halloween costume (in March)? Was it a joke? Or a fetish? In my gut I knew it was none of these things. My head swam with the implications of this one, singular image.

So, how does one respond—while on a date—when the father of one's children shares something of this magnitude, without warning or explanation, and then asks that we keep it to ourselves?

There was nothing to do but to quietly text back, *Okay. It will be okay. We will be okay. Can we please talk tomorrow, in person?*

Yes, she replied.

And then, with shaking hands, I turned off my phone.

On Prince and
Career Goals

The morning I heard the news that the iconic entertainer, Prince, had died, I felt compelled to listen to some of his music with my girls. I explained that he had died unexpectedly and much too young. I said I wasn't sure how he died (of course they asked), but that this was being investigated (which led to a whole other conversation about *autopsies*).

As it turned out, the girls did not much enjoy the music of Prince. "His music wouldn't appeal to everyone," I said, "but what an amazing gift to have your music loved by millions of people—to know that what you've created will live on long after your death."

I thought this was a perfect opportunity to discuss gender fluidity and the importance of not only being confident in who you are, but also of being accepting of others who don't conform to the norm. I showed them some images of Prince with his hair from long and wavy, to short hair with side burns, to afros, and with his clothes from feminine silk blouses and tunics to leather jackets and suits. He rocked whatever look he wanted to and never let himself be defined by—well, he never let himself be defined. I really wanted them to get the message that it's okay to be different and that in doing so, a person can bloom into something amazing—*themselves. Boom.*

Just as I felt I was really scoring a home run with this teachable moment, Beau said, "That seems like a good job to have."

"A famous musician? Yeah, that would be a great job!" I said.

"No, I mean cutting people open to figure out how they died." She pauses to consider this further, "It's like being a doctor, but if you make a mistake with the knife—at least you know you aren't going to kill anybody."

The Hawk

For nine days after Dad's heart attack, we held his hand, talked to him, and cried beside him as he lay, unresponsive, in his hospital bed. At his funeral, I said I felt this was a true gentleman's final act of graciousness—to allow us the time we needed in order to accept, if not to understand, why he had to leave us.

His prognosis was never good. He had been deprived of oxygen for too long. Looking back, I realize the doctors and nurses knew all along he was not going to wake up. The doctors were simply crossing their T's and dotting their I's—making sure they followed protocol. If I hadn't been in shock, I'd have recognized it sooner: the expression on all their faces revealing that they already *knew* the awful truth. They just weren't allowed to say it. Not yet.

My mother would admit only after Dad's death that she knew he had left us on December 27, the day he first collapsed. I suppose one can feel such a thing in their bones. After loving someone for fifty-five years, you just *know* when they are gone. She knew. And she stayed by his side, all day, every day. She never wanted to miss a moment with him. I also think that, whether she was aware of it or not, she wanted to afford my brothers and me the small comfort of coming to understand this reality on our own. She didn't want us to see her waving the white flag.

My older brother, Bill, is a realist. I wouldn't say he expected the worst, but he felt he needed to prepare for it. To him, losing Dad wasn't the worst-case scenario. Having Dad continue to live without the quality of life he'd have wanted—that seemed to be Bill's biggest emotional burden. He worried that Dad would come back to us in an altered state. He often sat on the floor in the hospital corridor, reading articles online about people waking up from comas with completely different personalities—not only physically and mentally impaired, but angry and hostile, the antithesis of our dad. He worried about us having to make decisions about Dad's future without being able to ask him. Bill didn't want our desire to hold onto Dad to hinder our judgment.

Ryan, on the other hand, spent his time reading about people who simply woke up—as if nothing had happened to them but a long nap. He wanted to believe in miracles. To be clear, we *all* wanted a miracle, but Ryan … he hoped for it with a raw desperation that was both beautiful and excruciating to watch.

I wanted to believe, too. I never wanted to leave Dad's bedside. At first, this was because I wanted to be there when he woke up. But after the hawk came—I didn't want to leave because I wanted to be there when he died.

One morning, before dawn, I was sitting on a metal folding chair beside Dad, holding his hand and resting my head on the edge of his bed. I'd say I was dreaming, but what happened was too visceral to be a dream. It was otherworldly. A hawk swept over my head, wings outspread. It flew so close to my face that I felt its feathers brush against my cheek. I believe the hawk was in fact a messenger from the spiritual realm (if not Dad's actual spirit), letting me know he was ready to leave his broken body.

I understood then that he was not coming back.

After that, it became incredibly painful to watch Ryan pleading with Dad to come back to us. I often had to step out of the room—my heart was breaking. I understood it was what Ryan needed to do. He wouldn't have been able to live with himself if he hadn't tried to get Dad back, and he did. He tried with everything he had.

One night when Ryan and I were alone, I gently suggested that maybe Dad *couldn't* come back. "What if he wants to, but he can't?"

I asked. "Maybe what he really needs to hear us say is that we love him, and that we are going to take care of each other. That we are going to take care of Mom. Maybe he is waiting to hear that he doesn't have to worry—that we will be okay."

This was hard for me to say, and—I imagine—harder for him to hear. The next day, though, he told me he'd thought about what I had said, and he agreed. So, while we waited for those final tests from the neurologist, we talked to Dad. We told him we loved him. We told him if he couldn't come back, we understood. We would take care of each other. We would take care of Mom.

We told him not to worry. We let him go.

My mother, brothers, and I all took different routes, and different amounts of time, to get to the place of acceptance—to the place of reconciling what we knew in our hearts to be true. At some point in our lives, we all must go through the processes of letting go, of grieving, and of beginning again in a new reality. The truth is, we really don't know, until we're there, how we will navigate a situation we never dared imagine. And there is no wrong way.

Beach Apocalypse

For the last twenty-plus years, my family has taken an annual trip to Boca Grande, a small island off the West coast of Florida. It is a trip we all look forward to with great anticipation. We start daydreaming about it right after Christmas, and count the days until May.

This year, the buildup has been different for us, of course. Taking this trip feels like something we have to power through, because Dad would've wanted us to go.

It is hard for me to explain how central Dad was to the whole experience. He was funny, in a smart, quick-witted way. He was warm, and everyone enjoyed being in his company. At the same time, he was never loud or boastful—he never needed to be the funniest in the room or the one with the best stories (although he had some good ones, for sure). There is something to be said about a person who is capable of being highly entertaining in humor and in intellect, but who doesn't ever feel the need to prove that to anyone.

I hesitate to say he was the glue that kept us together, because I think we're still stuck with one another (grin). But when you put a big group of people together—for us, "big" means up to thirty-five brothers, sisters-in-law, cousins, aunts, uncles, nieces, and nephews—there are a lot of personalities. I am lucky to have so many amazing people in my family; while some of us are closer than others, we all love each other. But my dad was so deeply loved by all, and he loved us all so deeply that, in his quiet, unassuming way, he was the heart of the group. We will all be feeling that void this year.

I had a dream the other night that the world was ending.

This isn't entirely new for me. Last fall I was having natural disaster dreams in which there was a flood or an earthquake and I had to save my girls. Those dreams made me panic. Interestingly, this dream about the end of the world did not make me panic at all. I was eerily calm, and completely resigned to the fact that the end was coming (I can't recall exactly, but I think a meteor was going to hit the planet, and Bruce Willis and Ben Affleck were unable to stop it.)

Since I knew we had only a few hours left on Earth, I thought at first that I would invite *everyone* over for a big party. We would flood the streets and spend the last hours festively. Then, I thought better of it, and decided I wanted to spend those last hours with the people who were most important to me—my family.

The dream ended with that revelation, which got me thinking. While I don't believe the world is going to end anytime soon, I'd be a fool not to realize how blessed I am to be gathering in Florida with the very people with whom I'd want to spend my last hours on Earth.

Gossamer Does Boca

Last night, Beau expressed that she wasn't sure she was looking forward to our upcoming family trip.

Some of our family had been together for a cookout the night before. She said she felt as though everyone was acting happy, but under the surface we were all actually sad. She said she felt anxious about being around a bunch of sad people who were pretending to be happy. I didn't know what to say.

Thinking about it today, what I want to express to her is this. Yes, Sadness will most certainly be joining us on this trip. Sadness so large and cumbersome that we should be required to purchase an extra seat for it on the plane. In fact, I imagine Sadness looking a bit like Gossamer from Bugs Bunny—a big, red, fury monster trying to squeeze itself into seat 12B.

The truth is, Sadness is not an entirely unwelcome guest. His presence is necessary on this trip. And even though he may get us a little choked up sometimes, it doesn't mean we have to let him run the show. We will laugh, and have fun, and enjoy each other's company—even with Sadness there. We won't be pretending in these moments. The happiness will be real, and everyone needs to know that's okay. It's how Dad would want it.

Next year, I'm hoping Sadness will be small enough to fit into the overhead compartment. That bastard costs a fortune in in-flight cocktails.

Kindness Is Free,
But It Might
Make You Late

My children used to miss the school bus quite often. This had much to do with frequent wardrobe dramas and generally not having our shit together by 7:15 a.m. This year, though, we are on a roll. We have not missed the bus once—until today.

One of my girls was very, very upset (read: sad, angry, stressed) this morning. She was upset about big things, small things—*all the things*—and she wanted me to know it.

I woke up with a headache, and after listening to her vent for twenty minutes I finally cracked. I *may* have thrown around the words *ungrateful* and *melodramatic.* Then she *may* have stormed up to her room and told me she would see me after school (in other words, she wasn't going). Then I *may* have said I would be leaving in five minutes with or without her in the car (a total bluff, I swear).

Downstairs she came, tears streaming down her face. Seeing this, I softened. I put my bags down and pulled her toward me. I needed to be the bigger person. I literally *am* the bigger person.

"Come here," I said. "I am so sorry we got upset with each other. I love you. I want you to have a good day. I want us *both* to have a good day." I felt her clenched muscles soften as she melted into me.

"I'm sorry too," she sobbed. "I love you."

Often being kind only takes a minute, and perhaps the willingness to set our own ego aside. Sometimes kindness also makes people late.

Busy

"Are you dating anyone?" he asks.

"No" I say, feeling a sudden and powerful discomfort.

"Why not?" he probes, not unkindly.

"I don't really have time. Between having the girls on my own five days a week and running a business ..."

My voice trails off, perhaps because I know this is a lie. You make time for what you want.

I don't share the words that rest on my tongue: *my heart is not available.* I don't share that I have packaged it up and left it resting on the doorstep of someone who doesn't want to open it. Could there be a better way to protect it than to leave it where it stays safely and tightly wrapped?

Sometimes, I think that the anticipation of something beautiful can be just as sweet as the actual happening. Sort of like the excitement we feel in anticipation of a vacation can be almost as sweet as the vacation itself. It occurs to me that this is a particularly convenient notion for those of us who have been disillusioned, disappointed, and wounded by love. Why? Because deep down we're scared that the reality of love will never be as sweet as the idea of it.

I spent twelve years with a person I never truly knew. I walked away from our marriage with two beautiful children, a smattering of scars, and some deeply painful questions: *If I never really knew her, did I ever really love her? Could she have really loved me? Do I even know what love is?*

Here's the truth: I am afraid. I don't trust my own heart to know what's true. So, there's safety here in the almost, the not yet, the someday. I see it now as it is—a hiding place, and hopefully a healing place.

Revealing this to myself doesn't change anything. Not today, anyway. Today, I'm much too busy.

Autopilot

A funny thing happens when you lose someone close to you. It takes a while for your brain to reset its "autopilot" feature. For weeks after Dad died, I'd pull into my parents' driveway, see my dad's car and think, "Oh good, Dad's home!" It would only happen for a split second. And then I would remember he is gone.

I know others have experienced this, too. They set one too many places at the dinner table, or turn to connect with a grin or a wink over an inside joke—only to remember their loss. Autopilot brain.

But after a while we move past this. We stop expecting to find our loved one in every familiar corner. Now, when I visit my mom and hear someone coming through the front door, I no longer forget for that split second that it *could not possibly* be my dad.

What I'm learning, though, is that with each new-old experience (something or someplace that's familiar, but we've not yet experienced apart), our autopilot brain needs a chance to reboot. Here, on this family trip that we are taking for the very first time without Dad, autopilot brain is in full force. I still expect him to come through the door with a coffee in the morning. I see someone walking down the beach toward me and think it is him. I expect to see him, drink in hand, as we gather as a group for dinner, or to watch the sunset.

Then, a split second after my autopilot brain fools me, the crushing weight of reality sucks the air from my lungs. I know my autopilot brain doesn't mean me any harm. Maybe it's slow to keep up with what it knows. Or maybe it just gets excited to fire those feel-good endorphins.

Either way, it hurts.

These Are the Days of Miracle and Wonder

The wonders of the ocean are endless and timeless.

Yesterday my cousin's daughter, Jenny, found a baby seahorse grasping onto a loose blade of eelgrass with its tail. It was no more than an inch long. As we stood there in the warm, turquoise sea, Jenny gently placed the seahorse into Beau's cupped hands.

Beau beamed and said somewhat breathlessly, "I could be in school right now, learning about decimals."

One More Last Time

Last night, as we were getting ready to head down to the beach for the sunset, I began to imagine what it would be like to have Dad back for just one more. He loved the sunsets. What if we could stand on the footbridge one more time with him, and watch "another day in paradise" (as he would always say) come to its glorious conclusion. I imagined us all clambering just to be near him one last time. In my imagination, when that last sliver of sunlight was swallowed by the ocean, Dad would vanish with it.

What we wouldn't give to have one more "last time."

The thing about last times is that we seldom know we are having them. We often take them for granted, arrogantly assuming we are entitled to many more—or perhaps not giving it much thought at all.

I know it's annoying when people say, "Enjoy every moment. It goes by so fast!" Exhausted parents are often cautioned of this by well-meaning elders as they wander, zombielike, through the grocery store, shirts caked in spit up, screaming toddlers in tow. But life is a freaking roller coaster sometimes. Life is chaos. Life is just *really hard* sometimes and it's all you can do to get through the day. One simply cannot enjoy every moment.

And so, I am not going to say, "Enjoy every moment. It goes by so fast!" What I will say to you is this: there are moments and experiences in life in which you are able to recognize *in that very moment* that *this* is a beautiful moment. That *this* is a moment you will always remember. That *this* is a moment that someday you will be willing to trade *anything* to have back.

Savor those.

The Loss in Me Sees
the Loss in You

Megan is eleven. She is with us on our family vacation. She lost her dad—my cousin, John—when she was eight. John was wonderful, except when he wasn't. Those who have loved an alcoholic understand what I mean by that.

We all mourned John when he died—though, sadly, we had many years to mourn his loss before he was actually gone. The disease took him from us long before his death. Megan wasn't able to process it in the same gradual way, of course, having been so young. I'm sure it felt sudden. And incredibly confusing.

During this vacation, two years after John's death and five months after my dad's, I know Megan recognizes the aura of loss and confusion in which my brothers and I are steeped. I can almost see her mind turning it over. *You lost your dad ... I lost my dad.* Every night down on the beach she writes sweet messages in the sand—notes to my dad and her dad.

I know it is a healing process for her, feeling this loss together with us. I am incredibly humbled, witnessing her within this connection. I am also in painful realization that we are so very spoiled, my brothers and I. We had so much time with our dad—and still, not enough—and Megan had so little.

None of us can ever give Megan that time with John—that charming, smart, funny guy she deserves to know and love. All we can do is wrap her up in family love and tell her that we understand, that it's okay to cry, that it's okay to feel sad and angry sometimes. Above all, we can reinforce for her that the ones we love will never be forgotten.

They were loved—and they will be loved—always.

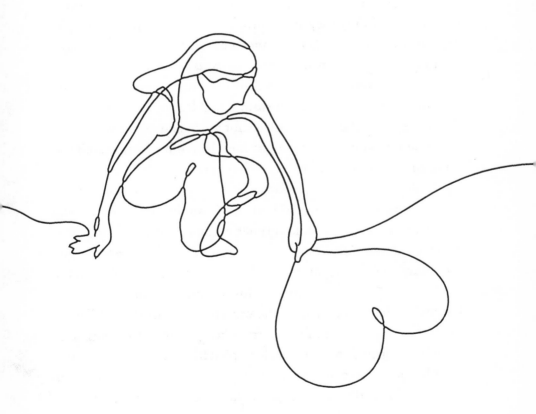

Protect My Child

We lost John to alcoholism. People never really say that. How many obituaries do we see that read, "He lost his courageous battle with cancer"—and yet, when someone dies from addiction, we are left to read between the lines.

There is shame associated with this disease—as if the person chose it. As if the disease of addiction is something a person can stop having, if only they are motivated enough or strong enough. True, many people are able to overcome addiction—but if you have an honest conversation with someone who has done so, they will almost always admit that they still struggle with it every single day.

For many, addiction is not surmountable. The demons are just too strong. I watched John struggle for years, and all the while, my whole family—my beautiful, tight-knit, incredibly loving family— watched this person that we adored disappear, bit by bit.

I will never claim to know what addiction felt like to John. But I *have* known—and felt, and seen—what it was like for those around him. There was so much pain, and guilt, and anger, and fear—and now, extreme sadness. Sadness for what might have been. Sadness for what this disease took from him. Sadness for what this disease took from us.

My heart breaks the most for his parents, my Aunt Anne and Uncle Ed. They loved their son fiercely and unconditionally. Everything they did was out of love—from being "fixers" to letting him fall in the hopes he would be able to pick himself up. That was the most brutal part—coming to grips with the fact that no one could help him. He had to do it himself. Ultimately, he just … couldn't.

John was sick, just as surely as if he had terminal cancer. It was not his fault. It was not the fault of his family or friends for not doing enough, not caring enough. I'm writing this here, and saying it over and over again, because while it is hard to accept, it is the truth.

Yesterday, I heard the song, "Lord Protect My Child" by Bob Dylan, and I just sobbed. *"He is young and on fire, full of hope and desire ..."* I thought about John as a boy, and all of the beautiful promise his life held. I thought about my own children—how I will always want to protect them, and how scary it is to understand that, at some point, it will be up to them, and to God (or the Universe, or karma, or whatever). At some point, it will be out of my hands.

Just like John once was, my girls are full of hope and desire. I choose to remember John with that beautiful promise—and to trust that he is at peace now.

On (Single)
Mother's Day

The girls and I got in late last night after our flight home from Florida. By morning, they had both made their way into my bed. As soon as Beau opened her eyes she softly murmured, "Happy Mother's Day." Ruby followed suit and nuzzled her face into my neck. We laid there for a while together—a warm tangle of arms, legs, and blankets.

They would soon be leaving to spend the day with Charlie. I really felt okay with that, despite it being Mother's Day, having been with them twenty-four hours a day for the past week. After all, Mother's Day is just a day—just another Hallmark-inspired gift-giving occasion.

Charlie came to pick them up and asked the girls if they had wished me a Happy Mother's Day (a polite gesture, of course). She did not offer up the sentiment herself. I wasn't really sure why that bothered me—after all I'm not *her* mother. I'm not even her wife, anymore.

Thinking about it some more, I realized why this omission struck a chord. It all comes back to the idea of being seen. As single parents, we have no one to witness us—not in all of the intimate and authentic ways that a loving partner could. No one sees all that we put into being a good parent. No one is there with us through the good, the bad, and the ugly of day-to-day parenting. We miss having someone to witness us at our best *and* at our worst. Someone who can therefore authentically and lovingly say, "You are a good parent." This desire for third-party validation is frustrating—I know I am a good mother. But it helps to have a partner who feels, without a doubt, that their children's lives have been made richer for having us as a parent. And while I believe Charlie feels this way about me, still I need her to say it.

But *why* do I need her to say it?

I thought about my mother, and how she had her "witness" with her for every one of her Mother's Days—until this one. My father was there through all that she put into being a good mother and grandmother, through the good, the bad, and the ugly. He could authentically and lovingly say, "Without a doubt, our children's lives have been made richer by having you as their mother." Of course, I have no idea if he said these exact words, but there is no doubt in my mind he felt that way. My mother's children and grandchildren feel that way, too.

And with that, the truth emerges. As single parents, let's not forget that our children ... *they* witness us. They see us—and love us—as we are.

Tightrope

Although I've been a single parent for the last three years, being without a partner felt heavier this year. More vulnerable.

Running it all through my mind in a stream-of-consciousness way—*Mother's Day without a husband, not so bad. Mother's Day without a husband* and *without a father, wounding*—I feel the feminist inside me cringe. But I think it's about traditional roles. The dad—and then the husband/dad—is the protector. The mom is the nurturer. But here I am, nurturing my ass off ... and where is my protector? He's gone. They are both gone—my husband-protector and my dad-protector—in entirely different ways.

When I got married, my dad "gave me away." They literally asked at the altar, "Who gives this woman?" Reflecting on it this way, it seems so perverse, even creepy. I know I was not a possession to be given away—but it's all about symbolism. I was Dad's only daughter. To "give me" to someone else meant something to him. It meant he trusted Charlie to love me as deeply as he did—to honor me and to protect me. To respect me. To keep me safe from harm.

And when all of that safety and caregiving fell away in my marriage, I still had my dad—the man in my life who made me feel safe and cared for. The best man I've ever known.

Going off on my own with two young children in tow, I certainly was strong—as strong as I could have been at the time. I was capable. But deep down, I always knew if I fell—*really* fell—my father would catch me. He would keep me safe. Now, I feel a bit like a tightrope walker who has suddenly looked down, only to realize the net—the net she always knew was there for her—has vanished, and it's scary as hell up here.

Knowing my dad was there made it feel safe to take risks. It made it easier for me to step off the platform, and trust myself to make it to the other side in one piece.

And, at the same time, I know that it was never really the net that kept me safe.

It was me.

We're Canaries

Did you know that miners used to carry canaries in cages down into the dark, scary places underground? When the canaries stopped singing, they knew it was time to get out, because the toxin level in the air was too high.

I never equated this bit of history to our experience as sensitive people until I read Glennon Doyle's book, *Love Warrior*. She describes saying to her roommate, "I don't think we're crazy, I think we're canaries."

My cousin, Lynette, is a canary. She sings her song without ever opening her mouth. You see it in her eyes, and in her smile. Sometimes, she stops singing, but only because she feels it all so strongly—all the invisible toxins that surround us. They can become too heavy for her tender heart.

Oh, but don't be fooled—she is strong, too. She is a *badass* canary. A world-traveling canary. A Machu Picchu-climbing canary. I asked her once how many countries she has been to; she said she wasn't sure, and that she'd have to think about it. I saw her start to count on her fingers ... and then get distracted before she could find the answer. Yes, it's that many.

Eyes are the windows to the soul, and you could swim in the depths of hers (though I warn you, prolonged eye contact is a secret pet peeve). To me, she is the personification of warmth. She is the type of person who goes out of her way to make people feel comfortable and important, from her elementary school students to the Uber driver. She listens, *really* listens, in a world where doing so seems extraordinary.

If you are lucky enough to be loved by Lynette, she will move mountains for you. When she can't do anything to help, she will call or text you every single day to let you know that she's here in the mine with you—and that, as dangerous as things seem, she is still singing.

Barnacles

"What are you writing about, Mom?" Ruby asks.

"I'm writing about how people might not think this shell is pretty," I say, holding up a pink scallop shell from our trip to Florida. "Because it's not perfect. You see, it has these barnacles on it—"

"Like how people are actually beautiful on the inside even though they might not be so perfect on the outside?" Beau asks.

"I think she means warts," says Ruby.

The shell is a vibrant, hot pink, but what I find the most fascinating about it is the cluster of barnacles attached. The barnacles have actually drawn some of the pink from the shell up into themselves.

Once upon a time, this scallop was a perfect specimen, new and unblemished. Somewhere along the way, the barnacles came along and attached themselves to it. In doing so, they have forever changed this scallop shell. They have become a part of it.

Much like barnacles, some traumatic experiences attach to us so strongly that they become a part of who we are—forever changing our very being.

Considering our own barnacles in the context of this metaphor, I wonder—just as we might pass by these altered shells, searching for something shinier, do we dismiss ourselves as broken, damaged, no longer worthy? Or do we have the perspective to realize that we— these imperfect shells—have actually been beautifully and irreversibly transformed into something of far greater depth and interest?

I'm Not Crazy (Yet)

Lately I have been having some issues—you know, mentally.

I can't tell if they are getting worse, or if I am just being harder on myself because I feel like I should feel better by now. It has been *five months* since Dad died.

I have been forgetting appointments, misjudging my schedule in ridiculous ways (mostly by thinking I have time for things I don't), not communicating well with others, having vocabulary and thought retrieval challenges ...

It seems like I vacillate between being in a fog, during which I have a hard time focusing, to feeling completely anxious, like at any moment I should be prepared to fight or flee. I am tired—*so* tired—right up until I lay down in bed. Then, my mind races.

Today, I had a meeting scheduled for late afternoon at work. This was a meeting with all of my colleagues—a meeting I would lead. Yesterday, I sent out an email reminder about the meeting today. Yesterday, I *also* offered to take two extra children home from my daughters' school for a play date today. I offered to pick them up and to keep them until dinnertime. I invited Charlie over to have dinner with the girls and me. "I'll make some soup," I said.

I fully intended to do both of these things—the meeting *and* the play date. And it did not register in my brain until today that this was, in fact, impossible.

When I realized my mistake, I felt stunned. It's a scary thing to feel like you are losing your mind, especially when you have a lot of people relying on you. So, I sat down and cried.

It wasn't a big deal to fix the situation. I asked for help. I called Charlie and explained to her what I had done. Bless her, she agreed to come over and oversee the play date while I led my meeting. I explained the mid-afternoon change of supervision to the children's parents. Everything was fine.

Except it wasn't.

I was completely distraught over the non-workings of my own brain. I sat down with my office colleague, Janet, and tearfully admitted that I was struggling. (It is entirely laughable that I thought she didn't know that already.) I told her what I had done, scheduling myself in two places at once, lacking any awareness of the conflict. I told her I was scared that I was losing my mind.

She said, "If you are aware enough to be worried that you are losing you mind, then you probably aren't."

I was listening.

She went on to explain that when we are mourning a loss, grief uses up so much of our brain function that other things take a back seat (whether you plan for them to or not). She said, "Stop giving your attention to things that aren't necessary. Stop offering to take care of other people's children. Stop offering to make dinner for other people. Just worry about taking care of you, and the girls, and your work. Sleep, eat, do what you need to do—and no more—for one year."

That was hard for me to hear. I like to do things for other people. It makes me feel good—and pulling back on something that feels good seems counterintuitive to the healing process. But I get it. At least for a while, until I feel steadier, I need to simplify.

Tonight, I looked up "effects of grief on the brain." I couldn't believe I hadn't done so sooner. I found an article that was so spot-on, I cried (again). Turns out, it's an actual medical fact that grief physiologically affects the brain. It affects concentration, memory recall, decision-making, planning, and organization. Reading this made me feel sane—and so relieved.

There it is in black and white: I'm not crazy, I'm just grieving.

You Shouldn't Have!

The tiny, octogenarian usher carried a tiny flashlight, which she kept pointing at my self-illuminating iPhone screen to see the seat numbers on our e-tickets. This didn't inspire a lot of confidence in her seat-finding skills, so when she walked us closer and closer to the stage to show us our seats, I was pretty sure she was making a mistake. My friend, Sarah, and I kept exchanging glances as if to say, "Seriously? Where is she taking us?"

This was particularly funny because I'd bought the tickets, and yet I was as incredulous as Sarah was that our seats could possibly be this good. (Later she said, "You should have seen the look on your face! Priceless!" I retorted, something like, "It's great when you are able to pull off a surprise *for yourself!*")

This sort of thing happens when you've been in a fog of grief for months. You do things, and you don't remember. Often this is stress-inducing or frustrating, but apparently it can also make for a nice surprise! Like discovering that at some point I must have believed that the Universe owed me amazing seats to see my favorite singer/guitar goddess and her guitar-god husband. I guess sometimes the fog ain't so bad.

What's Your
Pain Level?

Because we do not have the ability to enter someone else's body—their brain, their heart—and feel what it's like to be in there, experiencing their pain, there is no way we can possibly measure it. We cannot compare, nor should we try.

When a woman is in labor, the nurses will ask, "What's your pain level?" They want us to give them a number between one and ten—one being the least amount, and ten being the most pain we can imagine. When I was first asked this question, I remember thinking, "How can I possibly answer that? And will I be judged based on my answer? Is there a right answer for the amount of pain I should be feeling at this moment? Am I a wimp? Am I a freaking rock star?" I had no clue.

To answer the question implies that we know what a "ten" feels like—that we know how it will feel when have reached the maximum amount of pain we can endure. How could we possibly know? We don't. We can't. We can only answer the question based on the amount of pain we have experienced up until that point in our lives, and on what we imagine our limit to be. There is no wrong answer. Your eight might be my three. Her ten might be your five. We feel what we feel. And so, I try to find a place where I can allow my own pain to be what it is and someone else's pain to be what it is. Pain is both a universally shared experience and a completely individual one, and it is beyond our ability to measure or compare.

Let's not do that anymore. More compassion, less comparison.

What Is Grief?

Grief is love that has nowhere to go, they say.

I disagree. I think grief is love that wants to go *everywhere*. It streams from our eyes and threatens to burst from our every pore. We struggle and fight to keep ourselves whole—to keep from spilling ourselves all over the floor.

Holding Up
the Mirror

After Ruby was born, I found myself experiencing postpartum depression. I would wake up in the morning next to the most beautiful baby ... and the thought of a new day would bring me immediately to tears. It was bewildering and frightening.

At the time, the only person I had ever heard speak openly about postpartum depression was a woman named Monica. I got her number from a mutual friend and called her—a mere acquaintance, and quite out of the blue—openly sobbing. She received me with calm compassion.

Monica recommended that I see an acupuncturist/healer. She made the appointment for me, met me there, and held my baby in the waiting room while I was seen. I found this astonishing—that she would do this, without hesitation, for someone she hardly knew.

It can be hard to reveal our true, broken selves to others. Whether this is due to ego or to shame, I'm not sure. Maybe both. We want so badly to appear to have everything handled. I had guarded this illusion of composure and poise quite fiercely, even with my closest friends.

Desperation is the somewhat violent catalyst to great vulnerability. When we surrender to the fact that the only way to heal is to reveal our pain, we are forced to let go of fear of judgment. We have no other choice. I chose Monica as my lifeline, and therefore the genesis of our relationship was brutally—and I see now, beautifully—raw. She saw me for the mess I was, and it didn't matter to her. Or rather, it mattered to her in the most beautiful way. Even from the beginning of our friendship she saw the whole of me. She is intent on lifting me up until I am truly able to see the strength and the beauty within myself. Over these past eight years, she has been the kind of friend who always sees me for exactly who I am. And she loves me for all of my complicated messiness.

Sometimes I feel like Monica believes in me more than I believe in myself. Maybe we all need a friend like this. I believe I have been this kind of friend to her in return. We all need someone who is able to hold up the mirror—not to show us perfection, but to show us that perfection is impossible, entirely overrated—and, dare I say, boring. We all need someone who can say to us, "Don't you see? This is *you*. Beautiful, complicated, incredible you."

Manifest Some Damn Happiness

The Law of Attraction: we attract what we think about. The energy that we put out into the world is what comes home to roost.

When we are depressed, this is a scary concept. We might feel as though our depression is a self-fulfilling prophecy. We might believe that positive things won't begin to happen for us until we can muster up some positive energy. Yet, doing so feels like a Herculean effort at a time when we barely have the energy to get out of our own damn way.

When I learned about the Law of Attraction, it made absolute sense to me. I've been a positive and grateful person, and good things have happened for me. Lately, though, I've wondered—did good things happen to me *because* I was positive, or was I positive because good things happened to me? After all, it's easy to be positive when things are going well. But I get into a bit of a spiral about the Law of Attraction when bad things happen. I think, "Did I do this to myself? If I brought about the good things, did I inadvertently bring about the bad things too?"

I don't know the answer to this.

Maybe there is no such thing as the Law of Attraction. Maybe everything is random, and we cannot and do not have any impact on what happens to us. Maybe we are the arrows, not the bows. We don't choose our trajectory.

But I will say this: feeling good feels good. Feeling bad feels— you guessed it—bad! Run Spot, run. See Spot go.

As Monica would say, "Thank you, Oracle of the Obvious."

Geez. Here I am, feeling depressed—and knowing all the while that all I need to do to feel better is to stop feeling depressed. Duh. It's so simple! (There really should be a font for sarcasm). Then, along come the "Shoulds." I hate those smug bastards. They say I *should* do something to make myself feel better today. I *should* try to manifest some positivity. I *should* attract joy by feeling joyful.

For today, I am telling the Shoulds to beat it. I'm telling the Law of Attraction to leave me be. I'm allowing myself to wallow today. I'll manifest some damned happiness tomorrow.

Feelings Are Fattening

I usually don't worry too much about my weight. I don't even own a scale. I have stayed within a pretty consistent range since—oh, I don't know, my early twenties, when I drank beer like it was my job.

Lately, though, I've notice things are fitting—umm, not quite as comfortably. When I went for an annual checkup, I was shocked (okay, maybe not shocked, but definitely displeased) to see that I am presently fifteen pounds from my "feeling good about myself" weight. Oof.

During the week and a half that my dad was in a coma, and for a few weeks after his death, I had very little appetite. Then, something shifted, and I began to feel a perverse entitlement when it came to sweets and wine. It was if I was saying to the Universe, "You owe me this cheesecake, this brownie, this cabernet ..."

I guess people call that "eating your feelings." I know this is totally normal. However, as it turns out, feelings are some heavily caloric shit. Apparently, I've also been feeding my feelings to the dog. When I went on vacation a few weeks ago, the dog boarder commented that Louie—with his stocky body and short, stubby legs— looked like a bloated tick. (I know, Louie, life is cruel, and it turns out, feelings are fattening. I'm disappointed too. Now we know.)

Here we are, dieting together, Louie and me—equally miserable, and looking as wild- eyed as if it's been days since our last scrap of food. Louie adopts this expression immediately after having inhaled a meal. For me it takes at least an hour.

S.O.S.

When I understood definitively that I would be getting a divorce, my cousin, Eric, was the first person in my family I told.

S.O.S.! I texted. *Can you meet me at my office at 7? Bring wine.* Having no clue what I needed (besides, of course, wine), there was still not a second of hesitation, just, *I'll be there.*

A few hours earlier, I had been standing in front of the marriage counselor's office with Charlie. I hadn't known when we walked into her office that day that this was the decision that would be made. I was still in shock by what was revealed there. It was as if it had not been my own voice—but the voice of some stranger—that I'd heard utter the words, "I guess we're getting a divorce."

It was a beautiful October day—just like our wedding day had been, almost nine years to the day before. Charlie and I stood there for a few minutes on the sidewalk, not without tenderness. Neither of us knew what to say, so we just checked in about who was picking up the kids and went our separate ways, knowing our whole lives were about to change.

That evening, I laid the whole story out to Eric. I thought it would take him completely by surprise. He was quiet for a minute, but what he said next took my breath away.

"I'm sorry about your marriage, but to be honest, I'm actually happy for you. You haven't been yourself for a *long* time." He said this with such sincerity, I fell apart. *Of course* he had known. He has always known my heart, as I know his.

Eric is without a doubt the funniest person I know. Anyone who knows him, even peripherally, knows he is hilarious. He honestly can make a person laugh no matter what the circumstances—and sometimes completely unintentionally. (There was that one unfortunate funeral incident a while back …) He used to make my dad laugh like no one else.

The thing about people who are funny—I mean so funny that it is their most prevalent descriptor—is that sometimes one might underestimate their depth. But I know, without a doubt, that Eric would walk through fire for any one of us. In some ways, he already has.

You're Okay

It starts early. Well-meaning people tell us how to feel—and how *not* to. When we are little and we take a fall, our loved ones immediately tell us, "You're okay!!" before we are even given the opportunity to assess the situation ourselves. *Am I okay? They seem to think so. Maybe. But I don't feel okay. I feel scared, or hurt, or confused about what just happened. But they said I'm okay. I must be okay if they think so. But what if I'm not?*

Is it okay to not be okay?

We send a confusing message when we tell a child how to feel. When we tell them not to get so angry, so frustrated. When we tell them not to upset people with the truth of how they feel. Certainly, we should teach our children strategies for coping with life. We should teach them that there are appropriate times and places to fully express their feelings. We should teach them to be kind. But not at the expense of teaching them it's not okay to feel how they feel. We must teach them it's okay to feel *everything*. Not just the feelings that are comfortable for everyone else, or for them.

Sometimes I mutter under my breath, *you're okay*—even when I'm not okay in that moment. I do this to myself, and I do this to those I love. It was the first thing I said to Charlie when she revealed to me her foundation shaking secret—*It's okay. We will be okay.*

Is it? Are we? Is she? How could I possibly know? When I take the long view, I think—*yes, we will be okay*. But there's a whole lot to feel about the situation besides *okay*. We can't brush those feelings aside without allowing ourselves—and each other—to feel them.

When life gets hard, when my children stumble and fall, I want them to know they have permission to assess the damage for themselves. I will let them feel. I will listen. I will let *them* decide whether or not they are okay. They will know that whatever they're feeling—*that* is okay.

Be the Beacon

Lately my moods have been a bit … unpredictable. Sometimes I feel fine, but all it takes is that one tender remark or question to open up the floodgates. It's embarrassing.

A few weeks ago I was interviewing a job candidate and she asked me, "What is it like to work for you?"

In all honesty, I'd normally say working for me is a good gig. I'm even-keeled. I'm patient. I give unexpected bonuses or raises, and randomly buy meals or gifts for everyone. I'm supportive. I never say no to an employee asking for time off for a vacation or to make it to an event at their child's school. I want them to live a life of balance. I want them to be happy. I am often a sounding board and trusted confidante for their personal and professional struggles. They trust me.

"What is it like to work for you?" The question caught me off guard. To my horror, I began to well up. All I could think about was the time I've taken away from work throughout the past few months due to my own personal struggles. I thought of all the support and understanding I have needed from my co-workers. (Why is being a recipient so hard?) On the one hand, I understand that I need to give myself time—to be patient with myself. On the other hand, I know what it's like to be a light-bringer. Life is good when you're the bright and shiny one leading the way, spreading the light. I have *so* missed that.

To that end, I signed up for a sixty-six-minute Tattva Siddhi meditation that Saturday. The idea behind this particular meditation was to "become a beacon"—to shine your light and to feel oneness with others. *"You become as still and silent as a lighthouse. Grounded firmly on the shore, your presence becomes a beacon."*

I want to be a lighthouse. I want to be a beacon. No more of this crying-in-a-job-interview bullshit.

As the time to leave for the class neared, I felt myself wavering in my decision to go. Still sitting on my couch, I checked my GPS to see if I'd make it in time. Nope. If I left immediately, I'd still be three minutes late. Relieved to have an excuse—pathetic as it was—I called the studio to say I wouldn't be attending.

"Come anyway," they said.

"I'm not dressed properly," I said. "And there's no time to change." (Why was I trying to talk myself out of this?)

"Come," they said. "We'll set up a mat and a meditation pillow for you. Just slip in quietly."

So, I crept in late, and I found my mat. There were about twenty people in the room. Many of them were dressed in meditation clothing—complete with headscarves (I'm sure there's a name for those but I'm not up on the lingo). Some had yoga clothes on. And there I was in my ripped jeans, feeling a bit silly—or was it disrespectful?

"We will have our eyes closed for this entire meditation," the instructor said. (Oh, thank God.)

We started with some chanting. She said the phrases once; they were to be repeated three times each. Everyone seemed to know the words (not English, by the way) but me. I peeked to see if there was some sort of cheat sheet—something I'd missed because I was late. There wasn't, so I just listened, feeling a bit like an imposter.

The meditation would proceed like this—for eleven minutes we would take four even "sniffs" in, and one long breath out. The next eleven minutes we would take five sniffs in and one breath out—all the way up to nine sniffs. I assume the idea here is to become so focused on the sniffing that your mind can't run amok.

We started the meditation. I was ready to be a lighthouse … and then I heard it. Someone sniffing *so* loudly—sniff, sniff, sniff,

sniff, pause, *sniff, sniff, sniff, sniff, pause,* SNIFF, SNIFF, SNIFF, SNIFF ...

For the love of God. Really? Am I to be tormented by this sniffing for sixty-six minutes?

I cracked one eye open to see if I could spot the loud sniffer. I momentarily considered snuffing him (or her) with my meditation pillow. *Oh, the irony. Way to be a lighthouse, Bethany!* I stifled a giggle. *The whole point of this is to spread light and here you are making jokes about homicide? What is the matter with you?*

Okay, breathe. Let it go ...

And I did.

I let it go—and whether it took five minutes or sixty-five minutes and fifty-nine seconds, I don't know—but I felt it. I felt the light and the love fill the room. Everyone began to radiate it. It was palpable. And when it was over, we danced. The people in the meditation garb danced. The people in the yoga gear danced. And the formerly homicidal lady in the ripped jeans danced, too.

Ruthless

"Yes! I'm back, baby! Look out!" I grinned as I pass the dice to Beau.

"You are *just like Papa*," she said, smiling and shaking her head as she rolled her turn.

I was taken aback by the comment. It filled me with a sudden warmth. I welcome any opportunity to be cast in the same light as my dad—even if it is relative to insufferable game play.

God, it was so much fun to play games with Dad. While he was one of the kindest, gentlest, most selfless people you could ever know, game play was the one arena in which he allowed himself to be *completely* obnoxious—and we loved every minute of it.

What I loved even more than being compared to "Papa" was being gently reminded that my girls had the opportunity to know my dad. It is my intention to make sure they don't forget him. If I must do this by continuing to be an incredibly obnoxious and ruthless game player, so be it. It will be an honor.

No Souvenir Required

It wasn't the first time since Dad died that I'd visited the law firm he had shared with my older brother, Bill, and their two partners. I had been in the building on other business a few months before and had stopped in to see my brother. I remember walking into the office space and feeling the crushing weight of Bill's daily life. He was steeped in loss five days a week—imagining my dad coming around the corner every day, listening to their administrative assistants answer calls. *Did you mean William Harvey Jr. or Sr.? Oh, well I'm afraid I have some bad news ...*

I didn't go into Dad's office that day.

But here we were, at eight o'clock on a Thursday night, just Bill and I. I had come by to pick up some files I needed. The files were in Bill's office, so there was no need for me to go into Dad's ... but the sunset was hitting the windows in such a way that it gave the illusion that a light was on in there. It spilled out the door and beckoned me.

Of course, the light wasn't on, and my dad wasn't sitting at his desk, ready to call out, "*Heeeeyyyy*, Bethy!" (He's the only person on the planet who has ever called me that.) Tears poured down as I rounded his desk and sat down in his chair. I ran my fingers across his desk, a big, clunky antique with dents and grooves from years of use. I fondly remember hiding beneath this desk as a kid, playing with the mini cassette recorder he used to dictate letters to his assistant. Six months ago, my girls hid under this same desk, giggling and waiting to surprise their grandfather.

I took in the view from what had been his daily vantage point. The office itself was in a state of half-life. My brother had been slowly trying to clear things out, but Dad's pictures still hung on the wall, and his antique law books still filled the shelves. I opened the desk drawers—what was I hoping to find?

In the top drawer were three silver letter openers, along with his Notary Public embossing seal. I picked it up, found a piece of paper and pressed down, revealing the words William R. Harvey, Notary Public. I touched the raised letters and, for a moment, considered taking the seal with me. It seemed important—it seemed a part of him. Then, I thought how silly that was. Of all the things Dad was, "Notary Public" was not one of particular significance.

It's funny how we can get caught up in holding on to things— literal *things,* as if the possession of material items owned by a loved one will help us to remember. As if letting these things go will effectively strip away our loved one from us, item by item. But this is not true at all, is it?

My dad was not an antique law book, he was not a silver letter opener. He certainly was not an embossment stamp. The things he possessed that are worth holding onto are the bits of him that are found within all of us—my brothers and me, his grandchildren—as we are made from him. They are found within my mother, planted there through fifty-five years of devotion. They are found within every single person my dad touched with his kindness, generosity, and grace—the stories of which are still unfolding as people in the community continue to share their experiences with, and gratitude for, the wonderful man that he was. His indelible mark was left on us all.

Worrier Princess

"I'm a Worrier Princess!" Ruby proclaimed triumphantly.

"Do you mean, *Warrior* Princess?" I asked with a grin.

She laughed, "Oh yeah—warrior, not *worrier!*" It was good to clarify, because she does come from a long line of worriers. Lynette and I sometimes joke about the fact that if we can't readily think of something to worry about, it worries us. *There must be something I'm forgetting to worry about! Oh, God. Whatever it is, I bet it's awful.*

When I get up on my Worrier Queen throne, I try very hard to remember the best advice I ever heard about worrying. "Ask yourself one question: 'Is there something I can do about whatever it is that is worrying me?' If the answer is yes, do that thing that will help—do the project, fix the mistake, make the apology, whatever you need to do. But if the answer is no, then let it go. If there is literally nothing you can do about it, what's the point of worrying?"

Sometimes this exercise works really well. Other times I am presented with such a constant stream of potential disasters that worry becomes my default setting. This manifests itself in anxiousness—racing heart, racing head—and I become stuck in the heightened state of "fight or flight." And then, I become exhausted.

The poet Sabrina Benaim said, "Sometimes my depression is a firefly in the palm of a bear. Sometimes, *it is the bear.*" This is how I feel about my anxiety. So, I get it. I know that sometimes it isn't as simple as asking ourselves whether or not there is something we can do about it. In fact, sometimes that advice feels really patronizing and trite.

Sometimes what we need is to go to bed. Let the head and the heart rest—and hope that when we wake up in the morning, we will find that our anxiety is merely a firefly beside us on our pillow—and not a big hairy bear hogging the bed.

Grave Humor

I parked the car and walked toward the entrance of the church. It was a beautiful sunny day, and I decided it was time. I hadn't been there since Dad's funeral, so I decided the best way to find him was to retrace the steps of the funeral procession. His grave was still unmarked.

I don't remember a lot about Dad's service. I do remember making eye contact with Lynette as I walked down the aisle, my arm linked with my mother's, holding each other up. When my eyes met Lynette's, I saw that she had already been crying. I knew then that I wasn't going to be able to look at anyone for the entire service—not if I wanted to maintain my composure. Since my brothers and I would be giving the eulogy, composure seemed important.

After the service, we all processed up the hill—straight up and to the right, I remembered (or, at least, I thought I remembered). I knew he was buried under a tree. I remembered thinking that was nice.

And so, on this sunny day, six months after the event, I took those same steps up the hill—and there, under a tree was a new(ish) grave. I laid down on my back in the grass beside it, somehow imagining this was Dad's view now—the tree, the clouds, the blue sky.

I tried talking to him. I do talk to him now and then, and I wondered if talking to him there—where his body was—would feel different. It didn't. It felt forced, actually—like that was what I was supposed to do, because that's what they do in the movies. I heard some people talking nearby and I sat up, feeling a bit self-conscious.

Maybe they found it odd that I was lying down in the cemetery. I suddenly became amused by the possibility that I was actually lying next to the wrong grave, and talking to the wrong person. Dad always teased me about my sense of direction. He'd have a hearty laugh about me weeping over some other guy's grave.

I suppressed a giggle. It felt like we were sharing a joke, he and I—*and we were.* I realized then that for me, Dad is not here in this cemetery plot. It's more accurate to say that he is everywhere.

Later, I was telling my mom and Ryan about my thought—of Dad laughing at me as I lay beside the wrong body. Ryan laughed and said he'd had the same exact thought when he visited.

We are going to be okay, all of us. One inappropriate laugh at a time.

No Mud, No Lotus

"No mud … no lotus?" A quizzical expression crossed Beau's face as she read my new t-shirt.

"Do you know what a lotus is?" I asked.

"No."

"Remember that little pond down the road, where those huge, beautiful flowers come up every year?"

She nodded, "Oh, yes!"

"Those are lotus flowers. They grow out of the mud. So, the expression—*No Mud, No Lotus*—means that beautiful things can come from unpleasant things. Without the 'mud,' the beautiful lotus flower could not come to be."

She looked at me for a second and then blurted, "You mean, you think mud is *bad*? I *love* mud."

Once again, I marveled at how children's perspectives are so incredibly—and often unintentionally—insightful. "No mud, no lotus"—an expression meant to remind us that we must endure hard things in order for beautiful things to come forth. But what if we could think of the hard things as beautiful too? What if we could learn to love the mud?

It's a hard notion to accept—especially when our "mud" might not only be messy, but incredibly painful. How can we think of something painful as beautiful?

I guess it requires the ability to look *past* what we've lost. Maybe loss has inspired us to love more fiercely, to take risks, to be brave, to express ourselves like we never have before, to slow down, to savor, to pray, to be present, to take stock, to reevaluate, to cherish, to listen to ourselves.

In the nature-oriented preschool I own, we let the children play in the mud. We have outdoor mud kitchens just for this purpose, actually. Not only do the children play *so* creatively in the mud, but they also gain valuable skills. When parents remark at the end of the day about their children being particularly messy—or muddy—I sometimes will say, "That's a sure sign of a great day!" Or, when I'm feeling cheeky, "Good thing she's washable!"

What if we began to think of our lives as a sort of "mud kitchen?" At a minimum, we will probably learn something while we're mucking about. Perhaps, we will begin to appreciate the mud. Maybe we will actually enjoy it.

In the end, it's good to remember we are all washable, though getting un-muddied may take a bit of time and effort. And of course, there is always the lotus—a perennial reminder that like it or not, sometimes the mud is necessary in order to bring forth something of remarkable beauty.

Perhaps, that something beautiful is you.

Tidying Up

I confess, I haven't actually read Marie Kondo's book, *The Life-Changing Magic of Tidying Up*, but I get the idea (at least, as much as I can get the idea of a book I haven't read). The idea, as I understand it, is to hold each item in my hand and to ask myself whether it brings a feeling of joy. If it doesn't bring joy, I should get rid of it.

Brilliant. I'm in! And I'm dragging the girls along with me.

If you are a parent, you know that the moment you try to clean out a playroom or bedroom with your children, they will claim that *every single thing* brings them joy. My children are no different. That toy they have not touched in two years? Joy. That broken yo-yo? Joy. That doll with her hair chopped off and nail polish tattoos all over her face? So. Much. *Joy!*

Moving on to my own collection of things, I realized I had the opposite problem, particularly in my bedroom closet. That cashmere sweater with the coffee stain down the front? No joy. That dress that hasn't fit since 2005? No joy. Those expensive jeans hastily purchased after an extended bout with the stomach bug? *Absolutely no joy.*

Then, there's the kitchen shame. Let me tell you, very little in the kitchen brings me joy. As a mother, I feel badly about that. But also—where the hell does this stuff come from? Why on earth would I need not one, but *two*, bread loaf pans, when I have never in my life baked a loaf of bread?

In the end, we did get a lot done. The girls threw away nothing, but they did choose to part with about ten things, which they plan to sell at a yard sale and make millions. I'm not going to dash their hopes. It could happen. That wealthy, eccentric collector of incomplete puzzles—or of games missing important pieces—might show up and make them the offer of a lifetime. Then I'd look foolish for doubting my children's entrepreneurial skills.

Uh-uh. Not me. $50 for a half-finished coloring book? Totally.

I will admit that, as I purged and organized, I felt as if headspace was actually being cleared. I have about five areas in my house left to clean out. With any luck, by the end of the summer my head will be completely empty.

Waiting Out
the Storm

The storm started out innocently. Beau danced in the rain and stuck out her tongue to taste it. Ruby joined in the revelry, swinging her hips to the percussion sounds on the porch roof.

Then, the thunder started, and I gathered them up onto the porch.

I have always loved bearing witness to a passionate summer storm from the safe haven of a porch. Being within the storm, and yet protected from it. As the rain poured down around the roof in torrents, and the thunder boomed, the girls got nervous and wanted to go inside.

"You can go in if you'd like, but I'm staying!" I said with a broad smile, reassuring them. They gathered their courage and we huddled close together. Suddenly we heard a big crash of thunder and felt the bench rattle beneath us. We all screamed, and then laughed hysterically. They were thrilled. They felt brave—and safe—while witnessing something wild.

I suppose it's an important life lesson if you think about it. There will always be storms. We have to learn when to dance in them and savor them on our tongues—and when to wait them out from a protected place, huddled closely with the ones we love.

Big-Ass Swing Set

This may surprise you, but my mother has always worn the tool belt in the family. Whenever anyone was looking to borrow a tool—say, a table saw, or something along those lines—they would call and ask my mom, not my dad.

My mother tells the story like this. When we were little, she and my dad bought a swing set for us kids—an assembly-required, big-ass swing set. My dad was a busy guy. He worked full time, served on many boards, and was a town councilman for a few years. He did not have a lot of free time—especially big-ass-swing-set-assembly kind of time. So, the swing set sat out in the yard in pieces for … I'm not sure how long.

One day, my mom's friend, Polly, came over. Talk about badass. Polly did it *all* (and still does, in her eighties). She asked my mom what the deal was with the un-assembled swing set. My mom explained that we were all waiting for my father to have the time to assemble it.

"Why the hell do you need him for that?" asked Polly, incredulously.

Why indeed?

Mom and Polly dragged out whatever tools we had at the time (the collection has grown exponentially since Mom started asking for power tools for birthdays and Christmases), and they put that big-ass swing set together themselves. That day, a light bulb went off in my mother's head. She realized, "*I can do whatever the hell I put my mind to doing.*" So, she bought a book titled *How to Fix*

Just About Anything and started doing things like electrical wiring, plumbing, tiling, re-finishing furniture ...

One day, when I was in high school, I came home to a crashing noise upstairs. As I climbed the stairs and started down the hall, I realized the sound was coming from my bedroom. I walked in to find Mom in my closet, blasting a hole through the wall with a sledgehammer. She peeked her smiling face through the jagged hole in the sheet rock like Jack Nicholson breaking through the bathroom door in *The Shining*—*"Heeeere's Mommy!"*

She said matter-of-factly, "This closet is just taking up space in your room."

"Oh," I said, bewildered. (I mean, what does one say in this situation?) "Umm ... thank you?"

And so, whenever I fix things, or use tools of any kind—whenever I do something myself that I initially imagined a man might do for me—I think of my mother. When my girls create, invent, repair, or risk, I think of my mother. I know they will be strong, independent women—women who are not afraid to put together big-ass swing sets.

The Camp

My family has a house—the Camp—that was built in 1909 by a group of my great grandfather's friends. It has since been passed down, generation by generation, for over a hundred years. It is set up so that each family involved may use it independently of one another, and in turn. While I have no doubt it is special to every family involved, it is so quintessentially linked to my own childhood that it is sometimes hard to imagine it belonging to any family but ours.

The Camp is a rustic cabin, hidden amongst the pine woods, on the edge of a pond you'd never know existed if you hadn't known to look for it. We arrive by way of a bumpy, unmarked dirt road, lined with crumbling stone walls—reminiscent more of Vermont than of Rhode Island. As a kid, although we were only forty-five minutes from home, driving there always felt like entering another world. And it was. There was no phone, no television—and need I say it?—no internet. (That hadn't even been invented yet, kids.)

My father took time off each summer. During these vacation times, he wanted nothing more than to be at the Camp. He would never bring a razor with him, refusing to shave for the entire week. I remember looking forward to this uncharacteristic act of rebellion with glee; it meant Dad wouldn't go rushing off in a suit and tie. At the Camp, he was ours. I have so many fond memories of being there with him—of long walks in the woods, precarious trips in the sailboat, heated card games, and the comforting sight of him napping in a lounge chair on the porch.

As the years go by and technology permeates our lives more and more, it has become a challenge to preserve the simplicity of the Camp. But I try my best to give my children the same kind of experience there that I had. It is such a part of me—the pure love that I have for this place, and all it represents. The appreciation of nature, and of family. Taking the time to savor all that a slow summer's day has to offer.

I always pause for a moment, as I enter the Camp, taking in the familiar, rustic scent. I am filled with adoration for this place—a feeling which connects me timelessly to each generation that has come before me. I know that my love of the Camp is not only built upon my own memories, but upon the memories of those who loved it before me. When I am there these days, the sensation that my father is here permeates everything—as it should. I know I will always find him here.

Many years from now, my adult daughters may pause for a moment as they enter the Camp, taking in the familiar, rustic scent. I hope it will call to mind many of the happiest days of their lives. I hope they will be filled with adoration for this place—a feeling which will connect them timelessly to each generation that has come before. I hope they will know that their love of the Camp is not only built upon their own memories, but upon the memories of those who loved it before them.

And always—they will find me here.

Front Row Seat

"Can I go down to the dock?" Beau whispers into my ear, gently waking me in the early morning.

"Sure," I whisper back, "Can I come too?"

She beams. I go into the bathroom and splash some water on my face. When I reemerge, I see that she has already grabbed a wool blanket off one of the beds. She takes my hand. We venture down to the dock. The fog is swirling, hovering above the pond, waiting for the sun to shoo it away for the day. Taking a seat at the end of the dock, we spread the blanket around us both like a giant pair of wings—side by side with a front row seat to the awakening day.

Musical Chairs

When I was in my early twenties, I remember feeling really lost. I didn't know who I was—never mind who or what I wanted to be. At some point I decided that nothing was more appealing to me than having children and staying at home to raise them, like my mother had done. Perhaps this seemed like the safe thing to do—it was what had been modeled for me. (But that's a psychoanalysis for another time).

After that, dating became stressful. It was kind of like musical chairs, but instead of chairs being taken away one by one, it was the eligible men being removed from the game of my life. I saw my friends getting married, and I didn't want to be the one left without a "chair" when the music stopped.

The problem was, I fixated on landing in a chair rather than on enriching my life in other ways. I thought little about cultivating my own interests. I was certain that my life was going to revolve around my children and my husband—who, of course, was going to take care of us entirely—and life would be good. (Cue the feminist mob.)

Ultimately, I did find love and marriage, and my two beautiful children came into this world. I was a wife and a mother—but I had no idea who I was outside of those labels. I still didn't know who I was nor who I wanted to be as an individual. (It's safe to say, neither did Charlie, at that point.) Somehow, when my marriage unraveled, I found strength, self-confidence, and skills I never knew I had. I built a new life.

The beauty of where I sit now is that I don't need someone to create a life for me. When the time is right, I'll find someone to share in this very good life which I have already created for myself. It feels amazingly good to want, but not to need.

I have no regrets about the relationship Charlie and I had. No matter how things turned out for us, we made beautiful children. Children who are so loved. Looking back, though, at how I entered that marriage, and what I expected to find there within it, I'll say this.

I hope that, when my daughters feel ready to seek out partners in life, they will do so already feeling complete on their own. I hope that they will look not for someone to create a life for them, but for someone who will enhance the lives that they will create for themselves. I hope that they can build their marriages or partnerships upon the strong foundation of two people who want—but don't need—each other. And I hope that they will always trust that they are interesting, capable, and worthy people all on their own, independent of the labels of "wife" or "mother."

Perhaps I'll show them what that looks like, someday, with the right person. No matter what, I believe I've shown them that if the music suddenly stops, they don't need to scramble to find a chair—that it's best to stand on their own two feet.

You Only Get One

Looking at photos from the past year, I often think, *Look at me. I had no idea what was coming. How can that be?* I search my face for some indication that I had sensed the impending storm. How could I have been having such a good time?

It is disquieting—the recognition of the absolute fragility of our existence, and simultaneously of our (often complete) lack of awareness of that fragility. Oh, the arrogance. We make assumptions about how our lives will play out, when in reality we don't have any idea what may happen next—to us, or to the ones we love. Not only are we not in control, we are not promised any warning whatsoever when our world is about to be upended. Nor are we given notice of when our own time here will run out.

I know we can't live our lives in fear, worrying about what may happen next. We can't know, and we have to make that okay—the not knowing.

But *how*?

Reflecting on this recently with my Uncle Ed, he said "You only get one, you know." I nodded, thinking he meant we only get one life. But that wasn't what he meant at all. He went on to say, "You only get *one day*. You make that day the best day you can. If you're lucky, you get to string a bunch of good days together."

Not About Nutella

"So, you cut away the stems that are dying off," I explained to my girls this morning in our garden. "That way, the plant can put its energy toward the beautiful, new growth. See these new buds growing? Now the plant can put its energy toward those and it won't waste it on parts that aren't so good anymore—come here, you have some Nutella on your chin. Hmm, maybe that's what I'll write about today."

"You're gonna write about *Nutella?!*" Ruby laughed.

"Ha! No, not Nutella. New growth—and making way for it."

I've learned the hard way that we only have a certain amount of energy—physical energy, heart energy, and brain energy—with which to process our lives. When we give our energy to grief, anxiety, or depression (or all three at the same time), we have less to give to those things that make us feel good.

Many of us struggle to manage that trio: *Grief, Anxiety, and Depression.* They are a tight-knit group of visitors, and they *always* overstay their welcome. They are the uninvited and entirely messy guests who can wreak havoc on our lives. While struggling to evict those three thankless bastards, however, I have learned some valuable lessons.

I have learned to really sit with what feels good to me. I more easily recognize what works for me and what doesn't. I have learned the power of "no" *and* the power of "yes." (I have begun to say more of both, actually.) I've stopped doing things I don't want to do, just because I feel like I should do them. I've ordered up more of what feels good—which, for me, means doing *less*—which creates more space, more peacefulness, more quiet, more down time.

As I've begun to help these uninvited guests pack their bags—as Dad would say, "Here's your hat, what's your hurry?"—I've noticed a heightened awareness of the moments in which I feel completely contented and happy. Truthfully, I've always been good at taking snapshots in my mind of beautiful moments. Now, I notice more of them—and I swear I feel them more deeply. Even the really little things, like the feel of Ruby's small hand in mine as we walked through the yard together this morning ... I notice them more, these beautiful little bits.

So, back to the plant. The plant doesn't recognize its dying parts from its new and beautiful ones. It spreads its energy everywhere, equally. It can't help itself. Just as those of us with that awful trio of visitors cannot help but give our attention to them, pulling away valuable resources from the good stuff. Eventually, we will be able to be more discerning about where we send our energy. This process may look different for everyone, and sometimes—like the plant—we might benefit from a little help with pruning.

What Is Gratitude?

Beau asked, "What does gratitude mean?"

I replied, "It means being thankful. Not just for things, but for the wonderful people in our lives, for the kindness of others, for all of the beauty in the world—for everything. Noticing and appreciating—that is gratitude."

She looked at me and said, "So really, Mommy ... Gratitude is love."

The River

When I was a girl, I remember hearing someone use the word "grace" to describe my mother. "She has such grace," she said, with such admiration that I knew it was a significant statement. It impacted me, and though I'm not entirely sure I understood what "grace" meant at the time, I knew it was something to which I wanted to aspire.

Ironically, one of the ways in which my mother and I are very similar is in our lack of grace. We are both clumsy, and have a tendency to walk into things such as door moldings and furniture. We discover nasty bruises on ourselves, and have no idea how they happened. I like to think that's indicative of a strong tolerance for pain, but it's probably just that we bang into things so often that it fails to register as significant. By the time the bruise develops, we have zero recollection of the cause.

Of course, that's not what that person meant when she spoke of Mom's grace. They meant how she navigates life and relationships, not space. I aspire to one day be described in just this way.

To that end, this Buddhist quote is currently haunting me: *"In the end, only three things matter: how much you loved, how gently you lived, and how gracefully you let go of things not meant for you."*

How much you loved—yes, I love big and generously. *How gently you lived*—yes, I live with kindness and gratitude. *How gracefully you let go of things not meant for you* … well, two out of three ain't bad, right?

I've got a real problem with someone else deciding what is "not meant" for me—even if that someone is, you know, *God*. (Waits for lightning bolt to strike computer). Even though I know that "what is meant to be, will be," I still hate that expression.

A friend said … (okay, maybe it was a therapist. Ugh, fine, it was a psychic. Anyway, she said …) "You have to learn that the river knows the way, and it wants to carry you. *You are not the river.* Grab hold of a raft and let it take you. Otherwise, *you are going to get pulled under and die a terrible death.*"

She didn't actually say that last part, but it was implied.

I don't think I'll drown, exactly, but I know for damn sure that over the years I have expended a lot of energy trying to go in a direction that the river was never going to allow. Perhaps even more energy has been expended holding on—to a job, to a relationship, to a belief—clinging to the banks of the river with all of my might because I don't *want* to see where the river will take me. Why?

The first reason is fear. Even if I am suffering in my "holding on," at least I know what kind of hell I am in. What's that expression—"What fresh hell is this?" I don't want any fresh hell, thank you very much. The hell I know is much cozier.

The second reason is plain old arrogance (see also, stubbornness, asinine-ness), and believing that I know better than the river. *How can the river possibly know what's best for me?* I think. *I'll show it a thing or two.* (I have never shown the river a damn thing.)

Time and again, I've been reminded that the river *does* know, and it's not messing around. The river always takes me where I need to go, with or without my permission. The river is *much* smarter than me.

So, I'm working on it—on letting go gracefully of what isn't meant for me. One day, maybe I'll find ease in it. I bet life will flow a lot more smoothly then. In the meantime, I'll buckle up my life vest because those assholes—Fear and Arrogance—are clingy, and they are terrible swimmers.

Memory Loss

I forgot. For a split second, I forgot he is gone.

I was getting ready for a family dinner party and, just for a second, I got excited to see my dad. *Of course he's coming to celebrate Beau's birthday.* It passed through me like a flash flood of emotion— happiness, recognition, sadness, then guilt. How could I forget he is dead? It happened a lot in the beginning. Back then, the grief would hit me like a brick wall. This time though—seven months later—it was a weird feeling, the not-remembering.

It turns out this happens all the time to people who have lost loved ones. They pick up the phone to call them, or even begin driving to their house—only to remember their loss, and to subsequently feel a cocktail of grief and guilt.

How could we *forget* that we're grieving?

Here's how: our loved ones become a part of us. That doesn't go away just because they've had the gall to die. When we forget—for that split second—that our loved one is gone, it doesn't mean we've forgotten him. It's quite the opposite, actually.

The moments in which I forget Dad is gone simply prove that … he isn't.

The Canary
Takes Flight

"I need to tell you something while we are alone," Lynette said, nervously.

We were headed to meet some friends for dinner. Naturally, I assumed she was dying—so it was actually a relief when she told me she was only moving to the other side of the country.

Well played, Lynette.

I always want people to follow their bliss, their dreams—to go and do whatever their gut tells them to. As a preschool owner, I never get upset when one of my teachers leaves to pursue other interests. If someone feels called to be somewhere else, then that's where they should go. Onward!

I feel the same way about Lynette moving to California. Except I also want to wrap my arms around her ankles and force her to drag me with her as she goes.

No Regrets

Out of the blue, Ruby asked me if I went to my prom. "Yes, I did," I replied.

"Who did you go with? Did you go with your *boyfriend?*"

"Well, I went to my junior prom with a boy named Brian. He wasn't my boyfriend then, but I wanted him to be. Senior prom, I went to with a boy named Ryan. He was my friend."

"Did you ever get that boy to be your boyfriend?" she asked.

"Yes, I did. He broke my heart, though, in the end," I replied, perhaps a bit wistfully.

"Oh," she said. "That's sad."

I was quick with my response, because I meant it with all of my heart. "It isn't sad, actually. Not one bit."

"It isn't?"

"No—if he hadn't broken my heart, I never would have married your dad—and you, my dear, would not even *exist!*"

"Whoa," she said, mind clearly blown.

"That's the amazing thing about life," I said. "Sometimes you think what is happening to you is the worst possible thing, but good things often follow. There usually is a reason something didn't go the way you wanted it to go. You just can't see the whole picture until later."

She thought for a minute and said, "Kind of like Papa dying?" I felt a lump catch in my throat.

"Well—it's harder to think of a reason why someone has to *die,*" I said.

"I think I know," Beau volunteered.

"Really?" I said, more than a little curious.

She sighed and said, "When someone really important like Papa dies, it makes everyone around him appreciate everyone else who is *still here* a lot more. Before, I loved the people I loved—but *now*, I really, really love them *so much* more."

Our Decorations

A little girl I know was talking a lot about people's "decorations." Her mother thought she was referring to clothing or jewelry, but then she realized that her daughter was actually talking about the way people express their emotions. Their "decorations" are their feelings.

Children say the most profound things, if only we stop and listen. Her decorations—it's so true, isn't it? Sometimes we can't help it—our emotions are written all over our faces, and our body language screams of how we are feeling. We wear our "decorations" head to toe, and it feels amazing when we are adorned with love, joy, or gratitude.

But then there are the other emotions. The ones we don't want to acknowledge. The ones we would rather keep to ourselves. The ones we would rather *not* wear. We fool ourselves into believing these decorations aren't just as plain to see. We sometimes go to great lengths to try to hide them from the world.

But what if we could wear all of our decorations proudly? What if we believed that being able to fully feel (or wear) them all is a gift? Our vast and complicated wardrobe of emotions is actually what makes us feel alive.

Look at you—your decorations are beautiful.

Same as It Ever Was

When a person reveals that they are not who we'd always thought them to be—in the most obvious, fundamental way—it's hard for our brain to adjust. When we are asked to replace an ex-husband with an ex-wife, a sister with a brother, or a son with a daughter, it can feel like we are being asked to erase someone we love from this earth. It can feel like a death. At least, it did to me.

A few weeks after Charlie revealed to me that she is transgender, I planned to attend a memorial service for my father's cousin. We weren't close, but he was a lovely man and it was important to me to go. The service was at the same church where Charlie and I had been married twelve years prior. It honestly never entered my mind that this would be a problem.

The church is about an hour's drive from my house. As I got within a mile of it, grief hit me like a brick wall. I had this overwhelming feeling that the man I married—the father of my children—had died. He was *gone*. I pulled the car over and sobbed uncontrollably. I never made it to the service.

Over a year has passed and I have had time to process things. I understand now that this new woman in my life has not replaced Charlie. She has not killed him off. She is he. Or rather, he ... is she.

Charlie doesn't want to be different from who she has always been at her core. And she's not. She still makes me laugh like no one else, and she can still infuriate me like no one else.

Charlie simply wants to appear outwardly the way she feels inwardly. She wants her outsides to match her insides. And so, she is working toward that—toward being as authentically herself as she can.

If you ask me, she is incredibly brave.

Few of us have the courage to show the world who we really are inside. When I think about the masks we all wear, and the great lengths we take in order to *avoid* showing our realest selves to the world, I marvel at the courage it must take for her to simply be herself—to remove her mask when doing so opens her up to being misunderstood, judged, discriminated against, stared at ... or worse. People can be small-minded, cruel, even violent—and yet, subjecting herself to all of that hate is preferable to leaving the mask on.

Imagine that.

It reminds me of that famous Anaïs Nin quote, *"And the day came when the risk to remain tight in a bud was more painful than the risk that it took to blossom."* Charlie has chosen to blossom.

I am in awe of her. Which is not to say this hasn't been hard, or that it won't continue to be hard sometimes—for her, for me, and for our daughters. I have no illusions about that. It can be scary, confusing, and awkward for all of us. But we do our best. That's all we can ever offer each other in the end.

One evening, expecting Charlie and the girls, I looked out onto my front porch only to find a woman standing there with my daughters. It took a second for me to register that the woman with them was Charlie. I was seeing her for the first time, in person, wearing a dress, make up and heels. I felt my breath catch as the Talking Heads lyrics flooded my brain ... *"And you may tell yourself / This is not my beautiful wife!"*

I steadied myself, took a deep breath—and opened the door for my family.

Super Powers

The girls and I sat on our porch together, taking in the view of Narragansett Bay. I was enjoying my morning coffee while Louie, our lab, lay nearby, chewing on an enormous log.

Seemingly out of the blue, Beau said, "If I could have a superpower, it would be extra-strong teeth."

Laughing, I asked, "What would you wish to do with extra strong teeth?"

"Chew logs!" she exclaimed, with an expression that said, "*Isn't it obvious?*"

"Umm ... *why?*"

"Seems like fun," she shrugged.

"So, let me get this straight," I said, incredulously, "If you could choose a superpower—like flying, being invisible, mind-reading—you would choose to have *extra strong teeth?*"

"Couldn't I have more than one superpower?" she asked. Then, considering this further, she added, "I wouldn't want to fly, for one thing. Because I love to climb, and if I could fly, I'd just get *lazy* about my climbing."

Ruby interjected, "I would choose to be able to bring people back from the dead."

With a lump in my throat, I replied, "*That* would be pretty amazing."

Beau shook her head emphatically, "You can't do that. Their souls have already *left their bodies!* So, you'd basically be waking up *zombies.* That would make you a villain, *not* a superhero." Clearly, she has pondered this.

Offering an alternative, I said, "What if you could time travel? Then you could *visit* people who have passed away, instead of bringing them back from the dead."

Beau said thoughtfully, "Only if it was just to be able to *watch*, like a movie, not to actually do anything over."

"Wouldn't that be hard?" I asked. "If you went back in time and watched yourself in a situation, and you wished you had done or said something differently? Wouldn't that be difficult—to see your mistakes, and not be able to change anything?"

"No, because everything happened for a reason. Even the things we *think* are mistakes. We learn from things. Like … if I break my friend's leg—by *accident*—and she doesn't want to be my friend anymore. So, I meet a new friend who I wouldn't have met if I still had the other friend with the broken leg. If I go back in time and I don't break her leg, maybe she's still my friend and she has me hanging around some other kids who aren't very nice and I would never know I could have had this other great friend!"

"So, breaking your friend's leg—accidentally—actually kept you from falling in with the wrong crowd?"

"Exactly."

"You are very wise," I said, meaning every word.

Recapping, Beau said, "So … strong teeth, time travel *just to observe*, and—a third arm."

"A third arm?" I laughed.

"Yes, so I can lean back and relax with my two arms behind my head, and still have a free arm to pet Louie. It would come from behind me, like a tail."

"Ahh, a *butt arm*. Brilliant! You'd even be able to wave to people from behind as you walk down the street," I said.

And we, all three, collapsed with laughter.

In Which the
Reverend Angers Me

"How come you are so ungrateful?" the Reverend said to my brother Ryan and me, sitting in my parents' sunroom the day after my father died.

She didn't say those exact words, of course ... but that's what I heard.

Ryan, my mother, and I were meeting with her to make arrangements for my father's funeral. The Reverend had asked us to share some thoughts with her about Dad. After listening to us for a few minutes, she said to my brother and I, "You obviously had a wonderful relationship with your father. You know, as much as that makes this so hard, it may actually be easier for you to let him go. Easier than for someone who had a broken or nonexistent relationship with their father."

We were lucky enough to have had a wonderful father. We were lucky we had no regrets about our relationship when he died. We were lucky we didn't have any unresolved conflicts.

We were lucky.

But I can't tell you how far from lucky I felt in that moment. Her words brought me no solace. In fact, they made me a little angry. How dare she tell us that what we got was more than most? Her words, well-intended as they were, made me feel like a petulant, greedy child—to have had all this abundance and still want for more.

So much more. I ached for more with every cell of my being.

With time, I have been able to better appreciate her words. It is because we have so much gratitude for our father that we feel so wrecked by his death. At the same time, it is our abundance of gratitude for having had him that will save us. It makes it bearable, ever so slightly.

He left us so much to be grateful for. Not only the memories, but the many parts of him which influence our very being. Our father was funny, kind, generous, smart, and quick-witted. He was quietly confident, yet humble. He was extremely levelheaded, and of admirable moral character. He was affectionate, friendly, and warm. He was also forgetful, day-dreamy, and sometimes wouldn't have noticed if there was a wolverine in the room (especially not when he was doing a crossword puzzle). He loved to sing and to dance, and did both with debatable skill and undeniable enthusiasm. He was a hilariously insufferable card game opponent. And he loved his family deeply and unconditionally.

I see so many of these traits—these gifts from dad—in my brothers and me, and in our children. Some make me proud and some make me laugh, but they all make me think of him. And I feel grateful in my grief, because … we were lucky.

Snake Charmer

"It's beautiful, isn't it?" I said.

"What are we going to do with it?" one of the teachers asked me, as we looked down at the three-foot snake coiled in our school sandbox. It was harmless, but it obviously couldn't stay where it was. And I also didn't want the preschoolers to see any of us panic. After all, this is a nature school—we are supposed to teach them to love and appreciate nature, not to fear it. Even snakes.

As we stood there pondering our reptilian visitor, another teacher remarked, "Maybe we can have one of the dads help us."

I bristled. "Why would we need a *dad* to help us?"

"I knew you'd say that," she laughed.

Feeling sufficiently challenged, I grabbed a large push broom. I scooped the snake up (it obediently coiled itself onto the brush) and I walked it right off the playground into the field. I was determined to make sure that those spectating preschoolers didn't get the message that a group of women must wait for a man to help with such a thing. It was an empowering moment.

Still, I'm a bit of a fraud. There are definitely times when I do want a man to rescue me. My friend, Shane, can attest to that, having received this text from me just a couple of weeks ago: *Sitting in car at house. Dead Battery. Rain starting. All four windows open. Girls in a play in twenty minutes. Waterworks engaged.*

Oh boy. On my way, he replied.

Now you know my secret. Sometimes, I am a slayer of dragons and serpents (at least in the eyes of preschoolers), and sometimes I am a damsel in distress. In the words of Winston Churchill, I am "A riddle, wrapped in a mystery, inside an enigma."

Or, maybe I'm just like everybody else. Some days I feel as though I can handle anything put before me. And some days I want nothing more than for someone to swoop in and make everything okay.

More Alive

I've noticed an interesting dichotomy with regard to this summer. I almost feel guilty writing about it because in some ways it feels wrong and even perverse, but in other ways it makes perfect sense.

You see, I have had a wonderful summer—perhaps the best one in recent memory. How can that be? I've turned it over and over in my mind, and I have come up with these reasons.

I have stopped stressing over the small stuff. I know that sounds cliché, but I have gone through situations that have truly challenged me, and I have grown to understand my own strength. I know what I can handle—and it is quite a lot. Now, I recognize the measure of "upset" that is truly worth my energy—and what isn't.

I have been writing daily. I am expressing myself, getting it out. Expression leads to release. As my friend Monica would say, "What gets revealed gets healed."

In writing about my friends and family, I've been able to focus on what I most love about them. I would recommend this practice to anyone—examining what you love about those you love. And then telling them. It is beautiful.

At the same time, I have practiced adjusting my expectations of other people. Everyone loves in the way they know how, and everyone lives their own life in their own way. Having expectations about how that should look is a recipe for disaster.

Somehow, my love for my children has bloomed even more than I ever thought possible. This summer I have wanted to savor our time together so much more, to soak up every moment. I've wanted to freeze time. Perhaps this springs from my fresh awareness of the fragility of life—of recognizing that I have no idea what comes next.

I have been unafraid to say no if I don't want to do something. This has been incredibly liberating. All this time, I've been afraid of hurting people's feelings. But guess what? Most people don't want you to do things you don't want to do. We need to get over ourselves. We are not so important.

I have worked hard to create a work/life balance. Sometimes the lines blur—like when I have an urgent work matter to attend to during family time, or when I have to bring my girls to work with me—but for the most part, I am present at home when I am at home, and present at work when I am at work.

I've chosen time over money. I've opted to work part time this summer. In order to pay people to cover for me at work, I've had to rely on my savings to pay my own bills, rather than taking a salary. I'm okay with this. File that under "not stressing over the small stuff," and under "gratitude that I have savings."

There's no greater gift for my children than my time. I've tried new things and explored new places with them. We are making memories. I've been reminded what a treasure trove those will be for them, many years from now.

The bottom line is, I feel awake in a way I haven't been in a while. Not awake in a jittery, nervous sense, but in a *life is beautiful* sense. I'm so grateful.

Unexpected Visitor

Vibrant, literal dreams run in my family. There was a point when my mother forbade my father to watch spy shows (he loved *24* with Kiefer Sutherland) after he karate-chopped her in her sleep in order to protect the President.

Last night I dreamt we were having dinner on the beach, my family and I. Suddenly, there he was—my dad, arriving for the gathering as if we'd been expecting him. I ran across the sand and lunged at him with an embrace I can only imagine giving someone I never thought I'd see again.

He was bemused. You see, he had no idea he'd been gone. My family and I exchanged glances through teary eyes. Should we tell him that he died? Or that we thought he'd died? That would be quite a shock. I mean, what if we tell him he died and then he has a heart attack and *dies again*? Wordlessly, we made a pact to carry on as if him being here was an expected turn of events. He plopped himself into a beach chair as we tried not to suffocate him with our need to remain in close proximity. We didn't want our desperation to give us away. We soaked up every moment with him, because in our hearts we knew this couldn't last.

When I got up this morning and looked in the mirror, I saw the salt marks around my eyes. I'd been crying in my sleep, but they hadn't been tears of pain or sorrow. They had been tears of happiness. I had felt that lunging hug with my whole body. And while I ache for him to be here in the way he always has been—meaning, in his physical body—he is *here*. He can exist here. Timelessly.

Island Adventure
(Part One)

A few months ago, I looked on Airbnb for a rental in Maine during our summer vacation. I typed in *Maine, entire home, waterfront, dog friendly, under $200/night*. I didn't actually expect to find anything under those parameters—but, luckily, Airbnb has no sarcasm filter. To my surprise, a listing came up! It was a tiny cabin, on a tiny private island in the middle of a lake. Glorious!

One caveat: a person could not be hung up on little things … like electricity. Or plumbing.

Fast-forward a few weeks and the girls and I (and Louie, of course) were packed and ready for the four-and-a-half-hour trip to Annabessacook Lake in Monmouth, Maine. (Never heard of it? Me neither.) On the ride up the girls were quiet and sleepy, having been woken up two hours earlier than they had been all summer.

We found the meeting spot, but the hosts weren't there yet. We got out of the car to stretch our legs. Beau put Louie on his leash and decided to take him for a little walk while we waited. A few minutes later, I heard a loud crack, and looked up to see a thick, thirty-foot-tall birch tree come crashing down onto the dirt road ahead of them. I am not being overly dramatic when I tell you if had Beau been forward ten feet, that tree could have killed her. We were all a bit shaken. It was a (nearly) crushing reality check that nature is unpredictable—and we were about to be left alone on an island for three days.

The hosts arrived and ferried us out to the island. The cabin was bare-bones but adorable, with a sleeping loft and a real, old-fashioned water pump. (They were totally serious about the whole "no running water" thing.) We were reminded to boil the water from the pump before using it to wash dishes, and not to drink it. The hosts had provided us with drinking water. Baths were to be had in the lake (use the biodegradable soap, thank you very much). We got a lesson on how to use the composting toilet, which is basically an indoor outhouse. We brought a cooler with ice for our food. (No power, no refrigerator.)

The hosts left, and there we were, an island unto ourselves. We settled in, feeling like we were living in a Laura Ingalls novel, minus the prairie. We swam, caught fish and frogs, had lunch, and relaxed, all while peering off and on at the solar eclipse happening that very afternoon. (A friend had saved the day, supplying us last-minute with three pairs of eclipse glasses.)

Late afternoon, I was reading on the dock while the girls were swimming and playing on a rainbow lounging floatie we'd found in a shed. (I know, not very *Little House on the Prairie,* but neither were the eclipse glasses. We aren't purists.)

The girls suddenly erupted in a screaming match. "You get it! No, you! *You!*" I looked up to see the floatie ... floating away. It was already too far out for either of them to safely retrieve it. So, what did I do? I panicked. This was not our floatie to lose!

I'm either really awesome or really bad at "emergencies." You decide. Having already gotten fully dressed, I dramatically flung off my clothes and leapt into the lake in my underwear to rescue an inflatable piece of plastic. The wind had picked up and I got out pretty far before I realized, *this is how I will die. I will not reach the floatie. I will not make it back to shore. I will drown in my underwear in a lake in Maine because I couldn't fathom replacing a twenty-dollar floatie from Walmart. My children will be found three days later, motherless and wracked with a crippling, lifelong fear of floaties.*

Finally, I grabbed hold of the damn thing and dragged us both back to shore, where the girls were sobbing. Having previously witnessed my swimming skills, they had also been certain I was a goner.

Later, in an effort to restore my self-esteem after having emerged from the lake in a wet thong, clutching a rainbow floatie and sucking some serious wind (like, for an hour) I decided I was going to redeem myself by cooking us dinner on the fire pit. The girls and I got a fire going, and we cooked rice and chicken for dinner right on that pit. My earlier humiliation went up in smoke; I was a hardy pioneer woman once again. The three of us swore it was the best meal we'd ever had.

We had planned on s'mores and skinny-dipping under the stars after dinner, but by the time we were done eating and cleaning up, we were all full, content, and exhausted, so we opted for bed. Technically, I'd already been skinny dipping anyway.

Island Adventure
(Part Two)

I hope I'm not speaking too soon (for we aren't being ferried back to civilization until tomorrow morning), but I feel pretty confident that this adventure has been a success.

I did make some mistakes. There was, of course, the idiotic near drowning. I should have packed less food, more ice. A French press would have been well worth the cargo space. (I'd have given my left arm for a well-brewed cup of coffee this morning, rather than getting my coffee out of what was basically a mesh sock I'd found online.) We should have brought a few games, though we made do with cards. These are all small things to file away for the next adventure. Still, I've proclaimed it a success.

When traveling with children one has to expect that not every moment will be perfect. Siblings bicker, children get tired (as do adults!) and they don't always find "fun" the things that we think they will. Conversely, they often take great pleasure in things we never would have thought they would (often the simplest things, actually). My girls reveled in taking baths in the lake and using the old-fashioned water pump to wash their hands. They loved helping to make our nightly fires and lighting the candles inside when it got dark.

I've personally come to define a successful trip as one where I've experienced moments which filled me with gratitude for being right there, right then, with the ones I love. Those moments when

I thought, *this is happiness*. I felt many such moments on this trip, and I know the girls did too. I have asked them each what their favorite part was; they responded that it was being here, in this place, together.

Chronic

I recently read a piece in which the author and pastor John Pavlovitz likened grief to a chronic illness. I think this analogy is perfect. We may go through long or short stretches of time in which we are not plagued by our symptoms—a remission of sorts. Other times the symptoms are brutal, and relentless.

Lately, I have been feeling better. I have been working to bring my focus gratefully to what I had (a wonderful father) and to what I have (a beautiful life), and away from what I have lost.

But Chronic Illness will not allow me to believe that a cure is possible. In fact, Chronic Illness wonders how I have the gall to believe I'm better. It makes a point of reminding me that I will never be free from it. Chronic Illness knows that the best place to flare up is in the car—on long road trips especially. It knows I'm trapped, then.

It whispers, *Don't you remember what you've lost? Don't you remember that hysterical phone call from Ryan—the one that turned your legs to jelly? Don't you remember those nights curled up in the reclining chair because you wouldn't—couldn't—leave his side? Don't you remember the doctor with the smirky nervous tick? Don't you remember the cold conference room—the moment they said aloud what you already knew to be true? Don't you remember how you foolishly hoped, just for a second, that he'd wake up when they removed the breathing tube? Don't you remember how he died while your mother had been called out of the room? How he started breathing again, just for a moment, when she returned? Don't you remember holding his warm hand, knowing it was for the last time? Don't you remember, Bethy?*

There. There it is. Satisfied, Chronic Illness retreats again ... until the next time.

Heartless

This morning, as I reveled in my real electric-coffeepot-brewed coffee on my front porch, I felt fall in the air. A poetic friend wrote on Facebook, *"We left the windows open last night, and summer slipped out."* It was a cool sixty degrees, and I was reminded that "back to school" was just around the corner. The thought of summer coming to an end filled me with melancholy ... which is new for me, as I've always been a lover of fall. Usually, at this time of year, summer and its ever-changing logistics has left me exhausted, and I long for a simple routine again. I am an introvert, really. The inward turning of fall is a welcome gesture for me.

I considered what might be making me feel differently this year. I think it will be hard for the girls and me to separate into our own orbits again in a few fleeting days. I will miss them.

I am also keenly aware that with fall comes the countdown to the holiday season. I look toward that with great apprehension. It is hard to fathom a Thanksgiving or a Christmas without Dad.

I wonder, how does a family celebrate the holidays without their heart?

Survivors

It never felt as though my dad had a favorite amongst my siblings and me. We each had our own special place. I'm the only girl. Ryan is the baby. Bill is the eldest and dad's namesake. We all adored Dad, and we each experienced our own unique and tender relationship with him. Different as these relationships were, our initial shock at his death looked much the same. When I looked into my brothers' eyes, it was like holding up a mirror to my own pain.

But as we have moved through the nearly nine months since Dad's passing, I am noticing how differently we seem to be processing things as we acclimate to life after death. We all have different sets of life circumstances, different joys and stressors. We each seek different outlets for our grief and anger. (Exercise, writing, work ...) We each have our own triggers, too. I am not really sure if, in their daily lives (away from mine and my mother's), my brothers' pain is as exposed as it often seems when we are together. Or if the very act of being together bubbles it up to the surface for all of us. I guess there are some questions I've been afraid to ask ...

Do they have more joy when they aren't with others who, when looking in their eyes, mirror their pain?

Do they, like me, sometimes feel ashamed during moments of happiness—as if we are failing to don our respectful black mourning clothes?

Is their pain truly always as palatable as it seems? If so, do they suspect I may not have loved him as much as they did?

Did they love him more than I did?

Intellectually, I know that my brothers and I loved my father equally. More to the point, it isn't a competition, in which he or she who mourns the longest and the deepest wins. Dad would laugh (or, likely, *is* laughing) that I would need to be "the best" at grieving.

When I reign myself in from all of the crazy-making questions, I can see straight to the heart of it. Just as we each created our own unique and tender relationship with Dad in life, we must each create our own unique and tender relationship to him in death. There is no wrong way to do it. There is no timeline. There is no finish line.

There are no winners—only survivors.

Ed's Serenity

My Uncle Ed has been a sober and active member of Alcoholics Anonymous for fifty-two years. He has seen and heard a lot throughout those years, and he is incredibly succinct at cutting through bullshit and getting to the point.

You may be familiar with the Serenity Prayer, which is recited at the beginning of each AA meeting. It reads, in part, *"God grant me the serenity to accept the things I cannot change; the courage to change the things I can; and the wisdom to know the difference."*

Many years ago, Ed offered me what he referred to as the "abbreviated version" of the serenity prayer—"Fuck it." We had a good laugh, but he wasn't kidding. A lot of things can be dealt with by applying those two words.

The first is letting go. As in, this is not something I should be putting any more of my time and energy into. *Fuck it,* I'm letting it go. Enough is enough.

The second would apply to something for which I am willing to go the extra mile—to give more than I think makes sense, because it's so important to me. *Fuck it,* I'm doing this. I'm not giving up.

I think some of our greatest mistakes in life are the result of not making the proper distinction between these two varieties of "Fuck it." And so, I say, may we all recognize the times in life in which applying Ed's Serenity Prayer is wise. But, perhaps more importantly, may we never confuse the "letting go" Fuck-its with the "all in" Fuck-its. That would be a tragic mistake.

The Antithesis

As I stood chopping vegetables for salad, I asked my friend, Michelle, what her favorite part of the summer had been. She answered that she'd enjoyed spending days at a local pond with her children. It was quaint and small and picturesque, she explained. There was a wonderful sense of community there. Everyone knew one another and looked out for one another. It was comfortable, easy, and safe.

Then she turned the question to me. "What was the best part of *your* summer?"

I thought for a moment, and realized it was our island adventure in Maine, and that many of the reasons I liked it were the antithesis of the reasons Michelle had so enjoyed her days at the lake. Interesting.

I'll explain what I mean by that in a moment—but first, here's why I loved our trip.

It was just us—my two girls, our dog and I, alone on an island—and never was there a time when we were not enough for each other. I am keenly aware, having siblings and friends with teens, that there will soon come a time when our threesome may not be enough to entertain my children.

I loved the simplicity of our days there, for there was very little to do. The girls relied on each other and their imaginations (and sometimes cards, a canoe, or a fishing net) for entertainment. They also enjoyed participating in the tasks of cooking and cleaning, made more labor intensive (and somehow a bit more fun) without running water and electricity. The novelty of the water hand-pump, and the all-important job of tending the fire pit, seemed to fill them with a sense of purpose that perhaps chores at home are lacking.

Here's where I found the stark contrast to Michelle's experience at the pond. This trip was outside of my comfort zone. I felt scared—in the best possible way. We were never in danger (well, aside from the falling tree and my near drowning); mostly, I was scared that it would be a disaster. I was scared of failing. Being there made me feel brave, and it turns out I needed that.

You'd think that, after so much loss and heartbreak, I'd be seeking the safe, comfortable, community feeling of the local pond. However, it's all so obvious to me now: losing someone who we needed makes us want to prove how very capable we are of taking care of ourselves.

The Shrinker

Once, to endear myself to a man, I feigned indifference to one of the great loves of my life—Eddie Vedder, the front man for the band Pearl Jam.

It started because the object of my affection rolled his eyes and said something to the effect of, "Those meathead summer tourists, always blasting Pearl Jam ..." (He emphasized "Pearl Jam" as if they were the bane of his existence.) I nodded in agreement while I died a little inside from my lack of loyalty to Eddie. This may have been when I first noticed that I was willing to shrink for men.

It didn't stop there.

When I was on my first date with Charlie, I had been a vegetarian for a year or so. She wanted to order chicken nachos for us to share. I didn't want to seem high maintenance, so I neglected to mention that I no longer ate meat. (I didn't actually eat the chicken, just quietly picked around it. She seemed not to notice.) Later, I told my mother about our date and she said, sagely, "No good relationship starts out with dishonesty." I bristled, because I hadn't lied—I had just failed to offer my authentic self. Somehow, in my mind, that was better.

Over the next decade, this failure to be authentic and express how I was feeling—this shrinking—gradually sucked the life right out of me. One day, I woke up and realized that if I kept shrinking, soon there would be nothing left of me at all. I barely recognized myself. I was so very small.

When my life blew up, I had no choice but to stop making myself small. I had no choice but to stop shrinking and to rise—into the roles of business owner and single mother. I am stronger now. Independent. Full.

Confident as I might feel these days, when it comes to dating I'm afraid the Shrinker will sabotage me once again. Whenever I'm afraid to say how I really feel, I can hear the Shrinker whispering into my ear ...

Don't say that. Don't do that. He may not like it. Shrink, it's the only way to be loved. Shrink, little one. Shrink.

I know I keep being offered (yeah, I'll say offered) life experiences—relationships and interactions in friendship, business, and romance that challenge me—for the sole (soul) purpose of teaching me that it is okay to use my voice to express my actual feelings, even if that means saying things that the other person may not want to hear. Things such as, *Your words upset me. Your actions are unacceptable. I don't think you're being honest. I won't let you treat me this way.*

They call these repeating lessons our "karmic boomerangs."

So, Universe, please keep serving up these opportunities so I can continue to reinforce my backbone. Even though I know the Shrinker is wrong, she is very seductive. It is so easy to think she is making my life easier ... right up until the moment when I can barely breathe.

The Tethers Release

Today was my girls' first day back to school. Though we've been together all summer, they each seemed suddenly older and taller than before as they joined their classmates. At the school they attend, each first day back begins with a ceremony in which they welcome each child (in the whole school, grades one through eight) by name. It culminates with each of the eighth-grade students presenting one of the new first grade students with a rose.

Seeing the rising eighth grade class standing there beside the new first graders, I can't help but be keenly aware of the swift passage of time.

Monica dropped her daughter off for her first day of high school this morning. I noticed the same look on her face that I've seen on the faces of many parents dropping off their toddlers for their first day at my childcare center—a mix of hopefulness and fear. I always tell these new parents how important it is that they exude confidence—even joy—on that first day. Even when they are about to go out to their car and cry because their *baby* has started preschool, and the cocktail of emotions they are feeling is too much to bear. Even when they'll want to call us every ten minutes to see how it's going.

With each step our children take toward being autonomous humans, we feel more and more disoriented. We feel the tethers release one by one, throwing us off balance. We adjust our footing. We know there is no going back, and we want our children's universe to expand.

But also … Elizabeth Stone writes about parenthood that it means *"to decide to forever have your heart go walking around outside your body."* And so, off our children go, with our hearts in tow, eyes toward their next adventure. Perhaps not knowing that a part of us will always be tagging along.

Bless This Day

Since Dad died in January, I've been big on planning things to look forward to. I took a trip of sorts (sometimes two) every month from March onward. Having something to look forward to seemed to alleviate some of the misery I was feeling, albeit only temporarily. (As in, *I feel really depressed, but in two weeks I am going to Savannah with friends. Everything will be awesome then!*) And it *was* awesome—until, inevitably, I came back to my regular life, and Dad … well, Dad was still dead.

I hit some deep lows after these trips.

And then, there was the summer. The girls and I were entirely without a routine, with lots of fun adventures together. It felt as though the entire summer was a break from reality. The fact that this is the first fall I can remember in which I have not been longing—not even in the slightest bit—to get back into a routine, tells me just how much I have needed to escape from "normal." Normal without Dad is just … anything but.

And so, I find myself faced with the reality of normalcy—of routine—and I am trying not to bottom out yet again. So far, I'm okay. I'm optimistic, even. Instead of making big plans in order to distract myself, I'm just going to work on making today good. Tomorrow, I'll work on making tomorrow good. And on and on. I'm going to survive this fall and winter, not by skipping ahead, but by slowing down.

I have this verse by Mary Jean Iron in a frame on my dresser. Frankly, the sentiment is a difficult one to embrace when you're grieving—yet, I immediately loved it.

"Normal day, let me be aware of the treasure you are. Let me learn from you, love you, bless you before you depart. Let me not pass you by in quest of some rare and perfect tomorrow."

When you are doing your best just to tread water, blessing the day before it departs is just not happening. (Well, unless you are saying, "Thank God that's over!" but I'm pretty sure that's not what Ms. Iron intended.) I've realized there is no magic period of time after which I will be healed. I am forever altered; never again whole in the same way. Therefore, waiting for tomorrow, or the next tomorrow, or the tomorrow after that to begin to find peace and joy in daily life … after a while, that seems like a waste of a whole lot of todays.

Karate Lobster

I meant what I wrote yesterday about making each "today" a good day (rather than waiting for a better tomorrow to arrive). But today, ironically, I bottomed out—hard. This left me feeling like a hypocrite, especially after a dear friend texted to say how much she appreciates my advice. She called me "wise and wonderful," and I immediately felt like a fraud. Then, I reminded myself that, while I am writing to help others deal with life and loss, I am actually writing words of advice to myself, too. I am making this up as I go along.

Thank you! I texted back to my friend—from my hiding spot under my desk, where I'd been frantically trying to get a hold of my therapist. (Okay, I wasn't actually under my desk, but I thought about it.)

The truth is, I am much more Karate Kid than Mr. Miyagi. Wax on, shall we?

Within the last eighteen months, I have dealt with the sudden loss of my father, as well as the masculine-to-feminine metamorphosis of the father of my children.

I also feel a relentless emotional and physical pull toward my friend Michael, a man who is always just out of reach. While this isn't as impactful as the aforementioned events, I can't help but be influenced by his tides whenever we share the same orbit—which is often. It is continually, and somewhat inexplicably, disorienting.

Between the man I've lost—the man who has (in a sense) disappeared before my eyes—and the man who seems to forever leave me wanting, sometimes it feels hard to breathe, like the wind has been knocked straight out of me.

Today I have that uncomfortable-in-my-own-skin feeling; that wanting-to-crawl-outside-of-myself feeling. I recognize this particular sensation of discomfort. Recently, I've discovered it has a name—Post Traumatic *Growth* Syndrome. Perfect, right?

We often choose the image of the caterpillar morphing into a butterfly as the quintessential metaphor for personal growth. I think this is inaccurate. It implies a linear path from one point to another. A beginning and an end. I don't think we are butterflies. I've given it some thought, and ... I think we are lobsters.

(Bear with me, I promise it makes sense.)

In life, we don't just go through one period of personal growth—at least, I sure hope not. We have many opportunities to discover and redefine ourselves, often after periods of great struggle, discomfort, and vulnerability—some of which manifest in a desire to crawl out of one's skin. Which brings me to the lobster.

Many, many times in the life of a lobster, she becomes uncomfortable in her skin. She wants to crawl out of it. She sheds her old, hard shell so she can grow into a new, larger one—to expand her being. While the new shell is developing, the lobster is at her most tender. It is a period of great vulnerability.

Like the lobster, we continue to molt, over and over again, exposing our tenderness and vulnerability until we grow a new and larger shell. Then we wait, until it is time to become vulnerable once again. We are forever evolving into iteration ... after iteration ... after iteration of ourselves—each with a greater capacity to house our full, brilliant selves.

Let's not aspire to be butterflies at all. Instead, let's be lobsters.

The Dandelion

A dandelion caught my eye today in the forest. I thought it so beautiful that I snapped a photo. Looking at it closely, it is a miraculous work of art—a snow-white, intricate lace orb.

You may have noticed by now my love of metaphors. To me the dandelion is a perfect one for how we can label things in our minds as ordinary, not worthy of our attention—even as nuisances. But when we stop to really *see* them, we may find that the ordinary, everyday things are actually extraordinary and beautiful.

Having already been through a remarkable transformation, this dandelion is a delicate thing of beauty. Soon it will transform again, as pieces of it are swept far and wide.

Does the dandelion want to be completely dismantled in this way? Probably not.

(Is the dandelion capable of thinking about what it wants? Probably not. It's called poetic license. Humor me.)

I imagine it might say, "I've worked so hard to get where I am! Why must I continue to change?"

What the dandelion doesn't understand is that its ability to continually grow and transform itself is actually magic.

It takes some cajoling by the wind—"*Come, dance with me …*"

Eventually, the dandelion lets go. Perhaps not because it wants to, but because it must. And it becomes something new and splendid. All over again.

Papa Did This

We spent Labor Day weekend at the Camp with our family. It was a perfect way to kiss summer goodbye.

As we all sat together on the dock watching the most beautiful sunset unfold, Beau leaned into me and whispered, *"Papa did this."*

Some Fresh Hell

"... And so, I start chemo next week," my mother says, exhaling audibly.

My heart started racing the moment she told me I should sit down. Then it all became a blur of words like "tumors" and "biopsies." I struggle to bring this information into focus—to process what my mother is saying.

She has cancer.

She's known for a month. She went through all the tests and consultations before telling any of us. She didn't want to ruin the summer, she said. "You had so many fun things planned. Why would I want you to spend the month worrying and waiting for test results? Besides, it would have ruined my summer too. All these sad, worried faces."

"Mom, I can't believe you've been going through all of this alone."

"I wasn't alone," she says, "Your father was with me."

Practical Rage

I am on fire with anger. I finally understand the urge to break things. I want to walk into my kitchen, grab some wine glasses, and throw them to the floor. I want to watch them shatter into a million pieces while I scream.

But then I think ...

Brilliant, then you'll be angry and *you'll have shards of glass everywhere to clean up. Not to mention having to buy new wine glasses. Damn it! Can't you even rage without being practical? Fine, then. just crawl into bed and cry. Except we have no food in the house. Remember you made that really creative "trail mix" to round out the girls' lunches this morning? More like stale mix. We have nothing for dinner. Nothing to pack for lunches tomorrow ...*

And so, in my rage, I went grocery shopping. Because that's what a mother does when she has to feed her family, even when she is *the most angry* she has ever been—at life ... at the world.

I don't know whether to be proud or disappointed in myself for being incapable of wild bursts of emotion. Would it help to scream and rage and break things? Would I feel better? Or is it better that I weigh my anger against the potential of bodily injury, the inconvenience of clean up, and the nutritional needs of my family—and then settle on safety and lunch meat?

The Fog

I drive across two bridges every day, going back and forth to work. I love this picturesque drive. Today, it was a beautiful, clear and sunny day where I work. However, as I got to the bridge this afternoon, an illuminated sign read, "Fog ahead. Use caution." Indeed, as I drove up the incline of the bridge, the world began to disappear.

Living in a coastal town, fog is not unusual. In fact, I love the fog. It is quiet and soft, and lends itself to the imagination. However, today it struck me as ominous that we could so quickly shift from a beautiful day to the complete obliteration—of the world, and the road on which we are traveling.

It felt just *too* poetic. It was eerie.

It occurred to me that, when we travel through the fog, we must take a certain leap of faith. We literally cannot see what's ahead of us, yet we keep going. We may slow our pace, and proceed with caution. We may be justifiably leery of the potential obstacles in our path. But we never really doubt that the road will take us where we need to go.

Often, when we get to the other side, the sun shines again.

Grace Under Fire

My friend, Melissa, lost a brother at the Twin Towers on 9/11. I will never forget her panicked call to me after the first plane hit—when the world thought, for a moment, that the plane hitting the tower was a terrible accident. She knew her brother, Richard, was in one of the towers, but she didn't know which one, or which floor. As her family frantically tried to find out his location, the second tower was hit. Both collapsed. Richard did not survive.

This is only the beginning of the pain she's endured. Within two years of Richard's death, Melissa lost her father. During this time of fresh grief, she became a mother twice over. I can only imagine the strength it took to navigate all of this emotionally—the births and the losses, the tragedies and the miracles.

Then, almost two years ago, Melissa's husband, Jaime, was diagnosed with a rare form of cancer. He has been fighting so hard, and Melissa has been an amazing pillar of strength through it all. While Jaime has been in and out of the hospital for treatments, Melissa has been determined to keep life as normal as possible for their four beautiful children.

It happened to be the anniversary of the World Trade Center attack when I learned of my mother's diagnosis. Steeped as I was in anger and self-pity, I thought of Melissa—of her losses, her strength, her resilience, her *fight*. She is my personal idol of grace and grit, of humility and humor in the face of life's cruelties.

Despite all she has been through, Melissa strikes me as perpetually grateful. Her marriage to Jaime and the life they have created together is beautiful—and she never seems to forget that. Ever.

Recently when she and I caught up over dinner, she said, "You know, I am really looking forward to boredom. It sounds funny, but I'm serious. It will be wonderful when life just gets *boring.*"

We take so many things for granted, right down to the seeming minutia of our daily lives. What an amazing reminder to treasure it all, even—and maybe *especially*—the *boring* bits.

The Golden Threads

Throughout my twenties, I had this dark foreboding thought that my adult life was sure to be fraught with painful experiences.

This nagging bit of intuition was quite at odds with my generally positive outlook. I have been referred to as "Pollyanna" on more than one occasion. My older brother's friends took to calling me "Sunshine" after overhearing my fourth-grade teacher refer to me as such. Many of them still call me that, decades later. I have never been the gloom-and-doom type.

Nevertheless, I had this quietly simmering fear that, because everything during my upbringing had been so idyllic, so free of real angst, surely life was saving up to wallop me. After all, "into each life some rain must fall," and I seemed to experience nary a sprinkle. There I stood, holding this beautifully-woven tapestry of all the golden threads of my life, a privilege I was certain I had never really earned.

When it began to unravel, I remained calm. I patched it. I sewed it. I fastened knots to hold it together. Yet, despite my love for each and every golden thread, I couldn't keep it from unraveling. Today I feel as though I am lying in a pool of loose threads. I still love them so, but I can't help but despair at the state they are in. I run the damaged bits of silky cloth through my fingers, lifting them to nostalgically caress my cheek.

I know I can never recreate the tapestry I had before, for some of the most important threads are missing, or have been forever changed. Still, when I am ready (which, I'm afraid, is not today)

I will gather up my golden threads—even the frayed and knotted bits, for they are, in the end, the most beautiful—and I will weave them into something exquisite.

This time, I will know for sure that I have earned it.

A Witness

Somehow, I imagine the way I feel today must be similar to how an addict feels when she has relapsed. I was doing so well. I've worked so hard to regain my footing. By August I felt vibrant and grateful, even optimistic. But my mood shifted at the beginning of September. I thought it was the change of seasons that brought it on—but, looking back, I think it was intuition. Like tremors in the earth on which I stood, I felt the rumbling beneath the surface before I could see it or name it.

I have relapsed into a place of complete fatigue and helplessness. The worst part is that, like that relapsing addict, I feel ashamed. I know better. I am stronger than this. I have so many reasons not to be here again.

Fittingly, as I sit on my porch writing this, a dog is howling as if he is truly suffering. I've already investigated, soaking my slippers and the ankles of my pajamas in the wet grass as I trespassed onto my neighbor's property—compelled to make sure the dog wasn't trapped and wounded somewhere. He wasn't. He was just alone. We locked eyes through the window. He stopped howling for a moment, considering me. Then he resumed his sad, wounded song. There was nothing I could do. His pain was coming from a void I could neither fix nor fill.

Back on my porch, I am forced to listen to him in his grief. He won't stop. I think about drowning out the sound with some music, but somehow that seems disrespectful. So, we sit here, Louie and

I, witnesses to this other dog's suffering. Louie occasionally whimpers in sympathy.

Sometimes that's all you need, isn't it? Someone to witness you, until such time as things in your world make sense again.

White Flag

This weekend, I wallowed. I laid down my weapons. I waved my white flag—mostly from my couch, where I lay in my pajamas, subsisting on bread, chocolate, coffee, and wine.

I slept. A lot. I allowed myself to feel angry and sad and sorry for myself. It was a pity party of one, and I was the guest of honor.

When my kids got home last night, I was *so* happy to see them. I played games with them and I cooked us a good meal, but I was still inexplicably exhausted. I found myself counting the minutes until I could seek the safe haven of my bed once more.

This morning my inner voice whispered to me. *You needed that. I understand. But my dear, now it's time to pull yourself up. You can do this.*

A Box of Wishes

"These are antique candles," my mother said as she placed the half-melted candles into the top of the cake. I laughed, thinking she was making a joke.

"I'm serious! They belonged to your grandmother."

I picked up the box and looked at it more closely. *15 cents*, it read. Yup, definitely antique.

"They used to make candles that lasted a while," she said. "Not one-and-done like they are now. Imagine how many wishes have been made by your family members on these very candles."

It was a magical thought. Wish-granters, honored by being placed back into their box for safe-keeping until the next wish. How many people had wished on them? For what did they wish? Did their wishes come true?

We'll never know, but I do know two things for certain about these Harvey heirloom candles.

I know that every rendition of "Happy Birthday" that these candles have heard was surely appalling.

I also know that, whichever of us have leaned forward over these very candles, considering a wish—whichever of us looked around the room at the candlelit faces of our family, gathered together and singing hideously, but with so much love ...

I know they felt lucky, whether their wish came true or not.

Lines

Annette was my grandfather's sister. She was a well-regarded art teacher, a painter, a single mother of two sons, and a proud grandmother. I have thought of her many times over these past few months, as I have been writing and thinking a lot about gratitude.

One Thanksgiving, when Annette was quite old, my family and I sat around the dinner table to enjoy a beautifully prepared feast. My father encouraged us to go around the table, each of us sharing something for which we were grateful. As you might expect, everyone kept to a theme of family, of our good fortune to have one another (a beautiful home, wonderful food, etc.). I am quite sure a few of us got sappy and weepy, as Harveys are known to do.

Then we got to Great Aunt Annette. The table got quiet as we collectively leaned forward, not wanting to miss what was sure to be a sage bit of wisdom. She thought for a moment, and in her shaky little-old-lady voice, said, "I am thankful for the yellow lines in the road that help me to stay in the proper lane."

And with that, she picked up her fork and began to eat.

We looked around the table at each other and giggled. I remember my father, especially, getting the biggest kick out of that remark.

Aunt Annette loved her family. I am sure she was feeling just as grateful as the rest of us to be sharing good company, good food, and good cheer on that November afternoon. I don't think her response was the result of her really having to dig deeply to think of something for which she was grateful.

I like to think, instead, that she had gotten to a point in her life when she really did notice and appreciate the little things that made her world feel safe and comfortable—and that happened to include the yellow lines on the road. (Either that, or she was just messing with us.)

The Wind

Standing on my front porch with a warm cup of coffee between my palms, I assess the damage. Strong winds from a tropical storm off the coast have been lingering for days. The street is littered with small branches and leaves torn prematurely from the trees. Trash cans are overturned.

"Distress is the wind spirit of transformation," Michael said yesterday, when I told him how I was feeling. Now, with the wind whipping the hair around my face, his words seem eerily prophetic. I brace myself for the days (weeks, months) ahead. I have known of my mother's diagnosis for less than two weeks. She still insists on keeping it from the kids. She doesn't want them to worry.

"Mom, where are you?" a small voice calls from inside the house. Ruby peeks out the door and then steps out onto the porch.

"Is it going to clear up today?" she asks.

"No, not today."

She searches my face. "Are you okay?"

I force a smile, "Of course I am! We'd better go, or we'll be late."

Moments later, we arrive at the bus stop. I hug the girls and watch as they climb onto the bus and find their seats. I smile and wave as the bus pulls away, suddenly aware that I've been holding my breath. I exhale loudly, there in the parking lot, feeling raw and exposed to both the howling wind and the fearful anticipation of what lies ahead. I will be driving Mom to her first chemo treatment this morning.

I turn to see Michael standing there beside his truck, watching me, waiting to offer a hug or a few words of support. He's one of the few people who knows of my mother's diagnosis. As I walk toward him, he asks, "How are you?"

"Fidgety," I say, looking down at my shaking hands. We lean into each other. He wraps his arms around me. I try to relax into him, but it seems an impossible task. I step back to look him in the eye. "This is going to be hard," I say.

He nods. "I know."

I notice we are holding hands. I don't know if I grabbed his hand or if he grabbed mine, but it doesn't matter—neither lets go. I am grateful for this moment of comfort. I lean into him again and he wraps his arms around me once more. I want to hide here, sheltered from the wind. And from what lies ahead.

Hours later I find myself sitting beside Mom in the infusion center. Another loved one hooked up to hanging bags, tubes, and wires. I startle every time the IV beeps, flashing back to January in the ICU with Dad. In some ways it's harder to sit beside someone who is conscious. I didn't have to pretend to be brave or strong or optimistic while sitting beside my dad. He couldn't read the fear and sadness on my face, nor hear it in my shaky voice. I know I need to dig deeply for my inner strength for my mom, and for myself.

"I'm tired of feeling like a perpetual damsel in distress." That's what I'd said to Michael, when I told him about the diagnosis, right on the heels of grieving the loss of my father.

"Distress is the wind spirit of transformation," he said. And so it is.

The Pendulum Swings

Autumn made its presence known as a chill in the air, beckoning us to pull out sweaters and jackets. Then, suddenly, the weather turned, the sun shone brightly, and we found ourselves with an eighty-degree Sunday at the end of September. There wasn't a single cloud in the sky. The wind that had howled for days was reduced to a mere whisper. The only evidence of the stormy week we'd endured were the crashing waves and the smattering of tree branches strewn across roads and lawns.

It was a perfect reminder that, just as things can unpredictably go from beautiful and serene to complete upheaval, the reverse can also be true. Storms move on or dissipate, and we are left with calm in their wake.

As in nature, so in life: nothing is permanent. As a friend wrote to me recently, *The pendulum swings back and forth. Stormy to calm, harmony to disharmony.*

I suppose the true challenge in life is to appreciate the beautiful moments while they are being presented to us, without being resentful of what we've endured to get there and without being fearful of the next approaching storm. To stand boldly in the sunshine because we know it won't last forever. And to stand bravely in the darkness for this very same reason.

Stirrups

She walks into the room, a little bit of a thing with big blue eyes and red-framed glasses. She is the definition of "small but mighty." She sits down on her little swiveling stool and looks me in the eye. "You look tired," she says, and I burst into tears.

This always happens to me here. Perhaps it's the extreme vulnerability of lying in a reclined position in a hospital johnny. (Opening in the front, please!) Maybe it's because she was there both times I became a mother. She has seen me at my most raw. She has seen me at my most powerful and most powerless moments—when my children left my body and came into the world.

She hands me a box of tissues, apologizing that they are "the worst tissues ever." It's true: it feels like I am wiping my eyes with a paper towel. I'm annoyed now, because I don't have the energy for crying, but I can't stop, and accepting the tissues feels like an agreement to share what's happened. *We're in it together now.*

I recount for her the low-lights of the twelve months since my last appointment. She's quiet for a minute, then finally says, simply, "That's a lot."

"Uh-huh," I sniffle.

I am not sure what I thought she was going to say next, but somehow I thought it would be something more reassuring than what she *does* say, which is, "Do you have a good therapist? Sounds like you could use one."

She's got a point. I mean, at the very least a therapist wouldn't have such bullshit tissues.

After the appointment, I find myself with half an hour before I have to pick up my girls. There is a little beach around the corner from where the bus lets off. It's a private beach, and I know it will be deserted this time of year.

As soon as I get out of my car, I can smell that the beach is much more *fragrant* than usual. Tropical Storm Jose has churned up a lot of sea life and has deposited much more of it than usual onto the beach. What was typically a sandy beach was now covered in a bed of shells, rocks, and seaweed.

As I stand there, surveying the beach, it occurs to me that just as coastal storms churn the ocean, exposing things that were once hidden, so too do the emotional storms of life. Just as we can walk the beach after a storm and discover things previously hidden in the depths, so too can we discover things about ourselves that we never knew until they were unexpectedly—and perhaps, unceremoniously—exposed.

This new beach may not be as comfortable to walk on as it once was, but it is still beautiful, and even a bit more interesting—with stories to tell to those who will listen.

A Matched Set

Twenty years ago, my father had a heart attack and my mother had breast cancer, back-to-back. Obviously, they both survived that time around, but now it is all lining up too eerily. I can't help but think that maybe they are simply a matched set, meant to be together. The thought is both romantic and terrifying.

My mother is one of the strongest women I know. If she sets her mind to doing something, she will find a way. When it comes to cancer, she is already a survivor. If she doesn't believe she is ready to leave this Earth, I have to believe she isn't going anywhere—not without a hell of a fight.

So, we will have our weekly date at the infusion center, she and I. She will insist that I just drop her off and go home—or to the mall, or just … somewhere else (the chemo infusion takes three to four hours). But the thing about stubborn, strong women is that they tend to birth other stubborn, strong women. So, of course, I will insist on sitting there with her whether she likes it or not.

Big Enough

Last night, Beau and I were lying in her bed together. We shared a pillow, gazing at each other, our foreheads practically touching. I brushed the hair back from her face with my fingers.

"It's funny about love," she said, sleepily.

"What do you mean?" I asked, always intrigued by her mind's inner workings.

"It's just ... it is such a small word for something so big. It seems like L-O-V-E isn't a big enough word for it."

As usual, she's right. That one little word is *everything*.

War

Last night, there was a war in my house. Well, perhaps it was more of a single battle, as it didn't last long. It escalated quickly, and one of the sides beat a tearful retreat. I tucked the emotionally wounded party into bed and waited in neutral territory for her adversary to exhaust herself and raise the white flag. Which she did, in her own time.

Let me back up. My children love each other. They play for hours together harmoniously, scarcely aware of my presence in the house. However, sometimes, there are battles. Screaming, kicking, door-slamming battles. Battles in which words are used as weapons that cut deeply.

When these battles rage, I often find myself completely disheartened. I think to myself, *How can we ever achieve peace in the world if I can't even sustain it in my own home?* Anger—mean, angry words, in particular—makes me shut down and close off. This has never been an emotion with which I have felt comfortable; whether coming from me or towards me, it elicits equal discomfort.

Getting angry in response to anger isn't the answer, anyway. Anyone who has ever heard themselves yell, "STOP YELLING!" (guilty) knows how ineffectual and ridiculous it is. Sometimes I intervene, with the intention of staying calm, and I separate them. Whether I succeed depends on the day, the hour, and the nature and intensity of the battle.

I've also been working on getting comfortable letting the wars rage, to an extent. I realize that trying to keep the peace is often a futile endeavor. Maybe, instead, it is important that they learn how to express their feelings—even the ugly ones—in a safe environment.

I have found that after the dust has settled, and the gravity of those flying spear-like words has settled in, my children feel remorse without my assistance. It is important for them to recognize on their own when they've gone too far (even if it's after the fact), and to own it. To learn to admit when they are wrong. (How many adults do we know who still don't have this skill?) The girls don't need me to punish them, but to validate them—to say, "I know you were angry"—and to guide—"What you said was really unkind. When you're ready, I know you'll want to apologize."

In the end, they do apologize. They do this independently of me, and when they are ready. Unforced, their apologies are heartfelt and authentic, and are (usually) received as such. I hope they'll learn that apologizing doesn't make them weak. It actually requires inner strength—for what is harder than admitting when we're wrong?

As much as I hate the fighting, I don't want to stifle their fire. It will serve them well to be passionate humans—to defend themselves and others from injustices. I've personally spent too much time stuffing feelings down because I was afraid of them. They need to learn how to fight, how to apologize, and hopefully how to forgive.

Stardust

Tonight, I'm standing outside on the lawn of my mother's house—the house where I grew up. I have been spending a lot of time here lately.

I look up at the stars from the same vantage point I have so many times before. Stars that have always shone so brightly here, away from streetlights or city lights. So many times, I have stopped outside this house and marveled at the spectacle of beauty above me. For over four decades, I have been filled with a sense of wonder from this very spot.

For just a moment, gazing upward, it feels as though time and space are nothing—as if life and death are nothing at all.

Fear

Of all the emotions I have felt about Charlie being transgender, the strongest I have had, by far—and the one that has brought me more than once to tears—is fear.

I know her gender identity is not a choice. *Living authentically* within that identity *is* a choice, and she is bravely doing that. I marvel at her for being her true self. I can only imagine how hard it must be at times.

And—I am also afraid. I am afraid because people are cruel in heartbreaking and terrifying ways.

A few weeks after she came out to me, I spent a weekend in New York City. There is so much diversity in this city and I remember feeling grateful for all of the people who, like Charlie, were daring to be authentic even when that meant being different. We don't see a lot of diversity in Newport, Rhode Island.

But then, as I waited in Penn Station for my train home, I looked up in horror at the television screens as the newscaster announced the mass murder of forty-nine members of the LGBTQ community—a community of which Charlie has announced her membership. My head and my heart ached—and raced. I am ashamed to say that, in that moment, I felt angry at her for putting herself (and indirectly, our children) in harm's way. I thought, *We are living in a world in which being different is just not safe.*

I kept my fear and my anger to myself. I knew it wasn't fair to put that on her. Not when she is just trying to live her life the best way she knows how.

Today, in Las Vegas, there was a shooting spree at an outdoor concert. And I am reminded that we don't have to be doing anything particularly brave, bold, or different to be the victims of hate. We can just be children going to school, or people enjoying a concert on a beautiful autumn evening. We can be anyone, anywhere, doing anything, and our lives can end—because assault weapons are easy to acquire, and hate is a rampant disease.

So, we cannot let fear win.

I will be brave and encourage my children, and Charlie, and myself—all of us—to be who we are. To wear what we want to wear. To love who we want to love. To follow our passions. Because while we may not know what's around the corner, we can't live our lives in fear of it. We can't let hate win. Rather than losing heart—rather than hardening our hearts—we must keep offering them to each other, over and over again—even, and perhaps especially, when they are aching and broken.

Happy Non-iversary

Today would have been our thirteenth wedding anniversary. I don't regret my marriage. But I don't regret my divorce either.

Of course, divorce was never the plan. It never is, really.

I used to believe in marriage. Now I'd say I believe in *some* marriages. Seeing happily married couples makes me feel all warm and fuzzy inside. We were happy, Charlie and I, until we weren't. It was a long and difficult process to get to where we both knew it was time to let go.

I will fully own the fact that people I knew who got divorced prior to my own marriage's unraveling—I judged them. Not out loud, of course, but in my head—unless there seemed to be a reason for the unraveling that I deemed worthy.

I don't know what made me think I had the right to judge. Was it the ring on my finger? Was it because I was unhappy, too? Was I thinking, *Why should they get to start over when I'm stuck here?*

The truth is, not all marriages are meant to last. I know a lot of people will find fault with that statement, because the whole point of getting married is to make a lifelong commitment. Still, I'm saying it. We come into each other's lives for a reason (some call it a soul contract). We don't always know why, or for how long, the contract will bind us—but I dare say it isn't always forever, even if at one point in our lives we are convinced it is.

I am not advocating that people take marriage lightly. Really, I'm not. It is a serious commitment, and children add a whole other layer of responsibility. However, sometimes it is best for everyone involved (yes, *including* the children) when two people can admit that they no longer feel connected; that something is missing, and they aren't willing to quietly wither away together because they've made a commitment that has proven to be unhealthy for them both.

I am grateful for the nine years I spent married to Charlie. We had many happy times, and the times that weren't happy … well, I learned a lot about myself, and about life, during and following those times. I am also grateful for my divorce. I'm doing things I know I never would have done if I'd stayed married—things that have filled my heart and soul. I feel like I am discovering who I really am for the first time in my life.

I also want to say—although this may seem odd—that looking back, I am so grateful to have had the amazing wedding day that we had. It was a perfect day, and we were surrounded by all the people that we loved most. Several of these very important people aren't with us anymore, and so to have the memory of that perfect day, with all of them gathered to celebrate with us, is a truly priceless gift. For that reason, October 9 will never be a sad day for me.

This afternoon, when Charlie brought the girls home to me, I wanted to acknowledge the day, but "Happy Anniversary!" seemed weird to say. So, I just awkwardly blurted, "Happy October 9th!"

She looked at me quizzically. "What does that—oh, right. Shoot. Sorry."

Later she texted me, *I am sorry.*

I wondered for a moment if she meant she was sorry for forgetting our "non-iversary"—or for our marriage, or for our divorce.

After a while I simply wrote, *No regrets.*

She responded, *Same here.*

Focal Point

I have wanted to redo my bathroom for two years now. It had wallpaper with this horrible vertical stripe pattern that gave me a headache to look at. I never bothered to do it, though. It's a rental, after all.

Then, this weekend I saw a painting that I really liked, and decided that it needed to go in my bathroom—but not over the vertical stripes. So, I spent a better part of the weekend ripping down wallpaper (which is amazingly cathartic, by the way) and painting the walls of my bathroom.

I admit, I have never enjoyed house painting, I just don't have the patience for it. This time, though, I found it to be soothing. As I moved the paintbrush back and forth, I found time and space to think. I thought about how this one thing, this new piece of artwork, ended up quite literally coloring everything around it.

It's funny how a single thing—or event—can color our world entirely. It can make us change everything else to match it, often without our permission or awareness. This can be wonderful when the thing is something positive—like a new job, or a new love. It can make us want to raise everything else up to meet the vibration (or, in the case of my painting, the color) of this one, new thing.

Conversely, when the one thing has heaviness or darkness to it—for example, if we have our heart broken, get a scary health diagnosis, or lose our job, our home, or a loved one—suddenly everything else is colored by the darkness of this. Everything becomes gloomy. Presently, my mother's cancer is such a thing. When things elsewhere in my life begin to brighten, it feels strange—because the cancer is still here, and therefore it must darken everything around it.

Mustn't it?

Maybe not.

Maybe I get to decide what impact this illness will have on my world. Maybe I can deal with it without letting it become the focal point of my life—without letting it become the one thing which colors everything else.

No Hands

"You look like an angel today," Beau said to me as we were walking out the door this morning. "Except you have hands."

"Angels don't have hands?" I asked, amused.

"No, they don't," she said matter-of-factly. "That's why we have to do all the work ourselves."

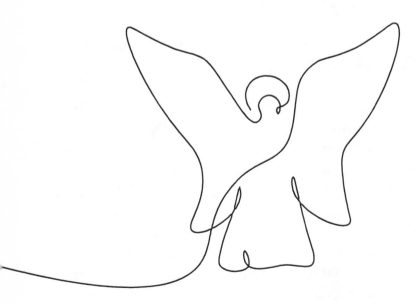

Violin Lesson

Last night, Beau felt very upset about her perceived lack of violin-playing skills. She said she was horrible at it, and that every note she played was wrong. There was a lot of playing of one or two notes, followed by sounds of complete despair. This went on for a long time. A *looooong* time. It was painful for all of us. Finally, I suggested she put the violin away and try again tomorrow.

I have been exhausted lately. And while I am blessed to have so many people and things that are important to me, sometimes it feels as though I am not giving any of them enough—or at least, not as much as I want to give. This makes me feel sad and tired and overwhelmed.

At work this morning and I was talking to my colleague and friend, Liz, about an upcoming event at the school. I was feeling overwhelmed by the idea of it. She quickly and easily broke it down for me, telling me what was already done (almost everything). Then, she asked, "What else can I do to make this feel lighter?"

I nearly reneged on having our friends, Michelle and Greg, and their three kids over for dinner on Saturday evening (something I'd planned a week or so ago), due to feeling over-scheduled. They offered to take a rain check, but when I said the girls had really been looking forward to having them over, Michelle offered to make dinner. "I'll bring dinner. No worries. Just breathe," she wrote.

I described my crammed schedule to Janet. From the bus stop to a lengthy meeting upstate, to the girls' school, to their dentist, then to a doctor's appointment—my day was jam-packed. "What'll

I do with Louie," I wondered aloud. I hadn't thought of him. He couldn't stay home alone all day, and but there was no room in my schedule for me to stop at home. "Bring him to me," Janet said. "I'll watch him."

After yet another meeting this afternoon, I was running late to the bus stop to get my kids. I called Michael, in case I didn't make it. "No problem. I'm here," he said.

While I appreciate all of this help from my friends, deep down it makes me feel incompetent, even ashamed. I *should* be able to do all of this on my own, and I feel as though I am failing miserably.

I managed to make it to the bus stop just as the bus was unloading. As the girls got into my car, Beau (carrying her violin case from today's lesson) announced, "Guess what! I am not actually terrible at violin! Turns out, I am just not good at playing it *all by myself.* It just doesn't sound as good as when I'm playing it with my friends."

I burst out laughing, hysterically. The girls seemed confused at first, until I said (between gasps for air), "After all that drama last night, it turns out you *are not actually terrible?*" The girls both started laughing with me. "I know!" Beau said. "All that drama for nothing."

It wasn't until later, as I crawled into bed, that I drew the obvious parallel.

I am not terrible at life—I am just better at it when I don't try to do it alone. And what a blessing that I don't have to.

All that drama for nothing.

Time Warp

The weird thing about death—or, at least, one of the weird things—is how it distorts time. It has been ten months since we lost my dad, yet sometimes it feels like just a few days since I last saw him.

As I write this, I am sitting on the couch in my parents' house. I can recall vividly the sounds of his evening homecoming. I imagined myself as little girl, running to the door to greet him, throwing my arms around him and breathing in the familiar smell of his suit.

He is still here, in every corner, in every space in this house. At the same time, sometimes it feels like he's been gone for years. It feels like he has missed so much.

Last night the girls and I ate at a local pub. Sitting there, I remembered that the last time we'd come here was with my parents. We were celebrating my birthday. *That couldn't have been my most recent birthday,* I thought. *That was less than a year ago. Dad has been gone longer than that.* I thought it had to have been my birthday two years ago that I was recalling. But it wasn't.

This will be my first birthday without him. I didn't necessarily see him on each of my forty-four previous birthdays (though I would wager to say I did on most), but without fail—from near or far—I was serenaded by him. Oh, I will miss that sweetly terrible sound so very much.

Crying Camel

The morning did not start out smoothly. One daughter irked the other, and before long they were at war. I tried to let them resolve it on their own, but at a certain point, I got pulled into it.

As the last proverbial straw was laid upon the camel's back (me being the camel), I burst into tears.

My waterworks surprised us all. I hadn't had a good cry in a while, and once the floodgates opened, I bawled. There were a number of things, of course, that contributed to my undoing—my lack of sleep, pent-up emotion about my mother's health, and the perhaps unrealistic expectation of a perfect morning—just to name a few. I felt terrible because the girls, of course, thought my tears were all their fault. I am all for letting my kids see me experience authentic feelings these days, but I know better than to make my children feel *responsible* for my feelings. And in that moment, I know they did.

I left the room to pull myself together. Beau came after me, asking, "Are you okay?" As I was nodding and blowing into a tissue, we heard the front door slam. We both knew this meant Ruby had left the house upset. I sighed, feeling defeated.

"I've got it," Beau said, and out the door she went—provocateur turned peacemaker, just like that. After I took a few minutes to collect myself, I went to see if I could help with the peacemaking mission. What I found were two little girls sitting on the front steps, arms wrapped around each other's shoulders.

I knew, in that moment, that we would all be okay, we three. Love is all we need.

Please Pass the
Mike & Ikes

Do you ever feel overcome by an emotion that you know is entirely … messed up?

On my lunch break today, I ran an errand. I glimpsed someone I've known all my life—a person who has not been well (physically, nor perhaps mentally) for years. I bobbed and weaved to avoid being seen and therefore having to have a conversation with her. I used to care for her quite a lot, actually. I still do I suppose, but in a nostalgic way rather than with any sense of a real connection.

The truth is, ever since Dad died, seeing her makes me feel angry. I feel angry because my dad—my incredibly youthful, seventy-year-old dad who took such great care of himself—is gone. And yet this other person, who seems to have checked out years ago, is still here.

I told you, it's messed up. I'm not proud of it.

With a dawning sense of irony, I sat there, shoveling Mike & Ike's (apparently, my lunch) into my mouth in a parking lot, stewing about how unfair it is that people who take *good care of themselves* aren't given any priority when it comes to life, and living.

But I know these things to be true.

First, we are owed nothing. Take good care of yourself because it feels good (or don't, for the same reason). We are not guaranteed one minute more (or less) on this Earth for doing so.

Second, every life has value. How dare I place more of it on my dad, just because to me, he was perfect? That's bullshit, and I know it.

Third, I have no way of understanding the path this person has been on, nor what she has been through. I have no right to judge. For all I know, she is thinking the exact same thing when she sees me: *Why am I still here when Bill is gone?*

For the last ten years of my grandmother's life, every time someone younger than her died, she'd say, "It just doesn't make sense that I'm still here." It seemed to be a combination of guilt—and, honestly, toward the end of that decade, resentment. She was ready. My grandfather had died twenty years earlier.

When she finally did pass away, my dad wrote her eulogy. I remember the last line clearly. Dad said, "I can imagine my father there greeting her—drink in hand—saying, 'Sugar, what took you so long?'"

I really do believe that we each incarnate onto the Earth for reasons we can only begin to understand while we're here. We all have our life paths or trajectories. Some of us simply get to be here longer than others, which can obviously be hard for those left behind.

So, what then? I still feel how I feel, regardless of the fact that I know it is wrong for so many reasons—reasons I am clearly capable of articulating and understanding. Sometimes emotion trumps reason. We just have to hope that time will heal us.

In the meantime, please pass the Mike & Ike's.

Vulnerability

One of the qualities I appreciate most about myself is my vulnerability. It is also the quality that causes me the most emotional disharmony within myself. It is both my superpower and my kryptonite.

I define vulnerability as a willingness to authentically share one's thoughts and feelings. When I risk being seen as I really am, and when I am honest about how I feel and what I want, I feel empowered. When I allow myself to be completely vulnerable with others, sometimes I even feel a high. The shadow side of this is that sometimes, after that barefoot rush of vulnerability, I feel foolish or even ashamed. There's nowhere to hide once I've pulled back the curtain.

Did I go too far? Did I reveal too much? Am I unlovable?

These dual edges of vulnerability are challenging, and also fascinating. I aspire to get to a place where I can be and say whatever I want, and never feel the sting of insecurity. (Oz, perhaps? Shall I ask the wizard for vulnerability without remorse? *My dear, you had the power all along!*)

Oh, to be able to stand in my vulnerability and to have the strength to not hold my breath in anticipation of the repercussions, the reactions, the self-doubt. To place my offering of truth before you and know that it is worthy.

I recognize that this is hard work. Perhaps the hardest work, for the *actual* definition of vulnerability is …

1. easily hurt or harmed physically, mentally, or emotionally;

2. open to attack, harm, or damage.

Who would choose this as a way to exist in the world? No wonder I'm exhausted.

Here's my truth—the reason it is so hard to be authentically vulnerable is because it is terrifying. Hence why I get a high from it; it's like cliff jumping or skydiving. It feels dangerous to be honest—to put myself out there and to risk that I will be rejected.

But the freedom in that sweet spot of truth is powerful and addicting despite the risks. This is where we truly connect—within our center of vulnerability. Within our hearts. The more we reveal our true selves, the more we understand each other.

It really is that simple.

Just Breathe

My brain feels a bit like it is firing on overload. I have so much going on that it feels like ... well, it feels like complete chaos in my brain. I am often in a state of anxiety about remembering everything I have to do. I write everything down, but it doesn't quiet the constant chatter in my head: *What's next, what's next, what's next ... don't forget, don't forget!*

I was talking to Monica yesterday, who mentioned having gone on a medication for Attention Deficit Disorder. I found myself hanging on her every word because when she was describing the calming effect the medications had on her, well ... it sounded like heaven. She has gently suggested to me in the past that I read a certain book about ADD, and that, umm ... perhaps I might fit the bill.

I might.

I had always thought of ADD as hyperactivity—as an inability to sit still, or to focus. I never realized that there are people with ADD who do not display outward symptoms in this way at all. They can actually appear outwardly calm, and are capable of hyper-focus if something really interests them. All of the busyness is *inside their heads*. This can actually look like dreaminess, like the person is lost in thought (and they often are). ADD can manifest as a lack of mental focus, and as distraction, irritability, disorganization, anxiety, depression, and exhaustion.

Do you know what else can manifest as a lack of mental focus, and as distraction, irritability, disorganization, anxiety, depression, and exhaustion?

Grief.

And so, I don't think now is the right time for me to seek an official diagnosis on the ADD front. For now, I am going to just try to be gentle with myself. It feels like I have a bowling ball sitting on my chest, and my mind is spinning—and I am pinned here, listening to myself spin.

I miss my dad, and my mom's cancer really has me scared. This is occupying my thoughts more and more.

I know I just need to keep putting one foot in front of the other. To keep using strategies to calm myself—writing things down to ease my anxiety about forgetting, taking space for myself when I can (hot baths are amazing in this capacity), trying to squeeze as many hugs and laughs as I can into a day (without forcing myself to be social when I don't feel like it … and I often don't feel like it, to be honest).

It will all be okay. I can do this.

Icemaker

After my dad died, I went to see a spiritual medium.

"Have you received any signs from your dad since he crossed over?" she asked.

"Umm ... I don't know. Maybe?" I said awkwardly. The truth was, I didn't feel like I had, not since the hawk visited me. Somehow, I didn't want to say that, though. I wanted to believe.

Ten months have now passed. And while my family sees signs of my dad in birds and in sunsets, he visits me through the icemaker.

Yep, the icemaker. (You can laugh; I sure am.)

The two summers prior to Dad's death, my parents stayed with me for a week or two while they rented out their house. I am so grateful for that time. When you live close to your family, you see each other more frequently, but it's typically in quick bursts—a pop in, a dinner. When you actually have family come and *stay* with you, it is a whole different experience. It's those little moments of being together for no particular purpose or duration—like coffee or a cocktail on the porch, reading or doing crosswords together, or impromptu dog walks. I loved it.

Except for the icemaker.

The damn thing *does not work*, but my father refused to accept this reality. Every time dad came to visit, he would turn it on. I'd inevitably walk into the kitchen and find a pool of water seeping out from the freezer. Or, I would open the freezer only to have crushed ice fall out all over the floor. It drove me crazy.

"For God's sake, Dad! I have ice trays! Why must the icemaker make ice? It clearly does not wish to!"

Now, every once in a while, when I open my freezer, ice will come pouring out onto the floor, or water will have inexplicably pooled there. There is no worldly explanation, for *I* do not turn on the damn icemaker.

Whenever this happens, I can't help but laugh and say, "Very funny, Dad."

Dear Mom

The thing about divorce is that, even when it is absolutely what a couple wants, it was never what they wanted.

Divorce is, in a way, a death. The more I navigate death and loss, the more this rings true. Divorce is the death of the life you thought you'd have with the person you thought you'd have it with. You may miss the physical presence of that person in your life, in your home. Even if the newfound space between you brings relief, you grieve the loss of the version of them you stood with on the altar. You mourn the person to whom you made a promise you can no longer keep. And so, just as with the loss of a loved one, in divorce, we grieve. We struggle to find our footing in a new reality. We rebuild.

After my separation, my mother struggled with how to help me. One night I sat down and wrote her a letter. I think, whether you are reading it through the lens of death or of divorce, it will resonate. Loss is loss.

Dear Mom,

Last night, I really fell apart. Retching, uncontrollable sobbing, to where I was afraid I might wake the girls. But I had to let it come. In a way, it was a welcome release, a surrender to some deep pain. I feel alone. I know I am not alone in the sense that I have so many people who love me, who want to support me. But at the same time, I am alone. It is me, and me alone, who needs to rebuild her life. This divorce, this death of a life I thought I would have, is a grieving process that I need to navigate in my own way. And I feel the weight. I feel the enormous weight of making this situation, this death, okay for my girls. They are grieving too. I have to walk the line of being human and honoring my feelings, while projecting—no, being—solid. Being reliable. Being okay. *It is hard, exhausting work.*

I know that you love me. I know you are trying to support me, and I am sure it is painful for you because you're not sure how. As I lay in bed, I thought about this. What does it mean to support me? What does that look like to me? Who or what has been the most helpful to me in these past few months? What gestures have meant the most?

Here is what came to me, and I thought I'd share:

Checking in, even when it seems like the effort is one-sided. I may not want to talk; I often don't. But it has meant a lot when people call, text, Facebook, e-mail—just to say "I'm here," without putting any pressure on me or placing any unnecessary meaning on whether I respond, when I respond, or the extent to which I respond. I might not answer the phone, I might respond to the message with a simple (and admittedly unsatisfying) "Okay," or "Thank you," but knowing you were thinking of me means so much.

Asking me to do something—getting me out of the house—but not being hurt if I say no. Offering again, even when I said no the last time, and the time before that. Not taking it personally.

Being okay with not knowing the details. I am still processing a lot. I have a lot of inner dialogues. I don't always want to talk about it.

Understanding that there may be people other than you that I choose to confide in, and not taking it personally. Knowing that it isn't that I trust them more or love them more, but perhaps their own personal experiences make them better able to relate to what I am going through.

Listening, without judgment or unsolicited advice, when it all pours out.

Understanding that I might be happy—joyful even—one day (hour, minute, second) and be utterly paralyzed with grief and fear the next. Rolling with it.

Letting me be selfish. Not mean, but literally self-ish. *I know that divorce is not the hardest thing anyone has ever endured. It may not be the hardest thing someone you know is enduring* right now. *But for me, in this moment, life is hard. It is confusing. It is at once excruciating, and full of hope and possibility, and frightening, and so very visceral.*

Give me a margin of error. A wide one. Let me fail to make time for people outside of my daily water treading. Let me fail to return phone calls. Let me forget things. Let me get defensive. Let me get sad, and angry, and giddy.

Give me a pass. Just for a little while. I am surviving, one day at a time.

Love, Me

A Virtual Family

On Sunday night, the girls had an impromptu change in their schedule by spending the night at Charlie's on a school night. When it came time for bed, Ruby was missing me. Thanks to FaceTime, I accompanied her into the bathroom to brush her teeth, and chatted with her while she changed into her PJs. I stayed with her as she got under the covers. As we were talking, Charlie came into her room and laid down next to her, partially filling my screen.

Charlie and I tucked her in together—they in the bed, and me on the screen. There we were, a "virtual" family. After we tucked her in, we moved on to Beau's room and did the same. A tender scene, to be sure. It triggered some sadness for me—but also warmth. I am grateful that we can comfortably share that kind of intimate moment together with our children, for our children.

I think there will always be a bittersweet feeling during the moments when we are enveloped together in our love for our children. No one else will ever feel what we feel for them—the absolute awe and gratitude for their very existence. There is often an exchanged glance between us in moments like these, and I know we are both thinking the same thing—*I'm sorry. I wish things were different.*

At this point, the regret isn't about our relationship. It is about our family. We wish things were different for them. The truth is, though, that our children have moved on. They have embraced the new normal. What seems to matter most to them is that Charlie and I authentically care about each other. When they see us interact and communicate with each other in a warm and respectful way, they are happy.

The children notice *everything*. Any modicum of disharmony is felt in their bones. Our mere tremors can rock their very foundation. Sometimes it can't be helped, the disharmony. We've been through so much, Charlie and I. Some of it has been too painful to hide, despite our best efforts.

Though the initial separation was amicable, the actual process of divorce was hard on us. We started with a mediator, but ultimately had to rely on lawyers to help us. This caused us both to load on the armor (never a good thing). We learned the hard way how important it is to keep communicating with each other, and to avoid allowing other people to speak for us whenever possible. Too much can be lost in translation, especially when we already have our guard up.

Finding my voice and working on creating healthy boundaries in this post-divorce relationship has in many ways made it much harder to navigate than the marital relationship ever was. There are times when I don't know how we will ever recover, but we always do.

Fancy Dive

I stand in front of Michael, naked and dripping wet. He glances up at me, reading glasses perched on the end of his nose. He is about to speak, when his phone lights up with a text message. "I have to get this," he says dismissively.

I quietly walk away, wrapping myself in a towel and gathering up my clothes. I am fully dressed when I notice, at last, he is looking at me.

Without pause, I walk over to him and begin removing my clothes, slowly and deliberately baring myself to him all over again. I turn and walk toward the diving platform. I ascend the ladder and stand on the edge of the diving board. I smile at him. He smiles back. I fly into the air, executing an elaborate dive. I come up for air and look to see his reaction.

He isn't watching. He didn't see.

I swim to the edge of the pool and lift myself out. I grab my towel, dry off, and get dressed again. He doesn't look up.

Then, I feel his eyes on me. I walk over to him and start to undress once more. This scene plays out over and over, always the same—except each dive becomes more elaborate than the last. Perhaps a Backflip? A Jackknife? Double gainer loop-de-loop? More splash? Less splash?

Still, he is unimpressed.

I wake up alone in my bed, feeling entirely exposed and ... ashamed. You see, I adore this man. And I dive off the platform for him, again and again.

"Look at me," I whisper. I plead. I shout. I *scream!* "Aren't I smart? Aren't I funny? Aren't I kind? Aren't I beautiful? Aren't I *enough?"* I keep climbing the ladder, walking the plank, holding my breath and hoping—hoping that, this time, he'll see me.

But he won't.

For a long time, he has been saying to me, "I am not the man for you." But all that did was spur me to take up the challenge. *What makes you think you know what's best for me? I'll decide that, thank you very much!* In reality, perhaps what he should have said—what he meant—was, "You are not the right woman for me."

I adore him still. I want so much happiness for him. I am grateful for the fire he lit in me, long after I had forgotten how that felt. Nevertheless, it is time to recognize that he will not be the one to sustain this fire.

And that I will not be the one to sustain his. Someday the right woman will appear before him, and he will look up, and he will see her. And as much as I want that for him, I just can't bear to be standing here—naked on the diving board—when it happens.

I'm not angry. I *can't* be angry at someone for not loving me in the way I'd hoped. I don't even consider my endless pining to have been a waste of my time. In a way, his waxing and waning disinterest protected me from myself. After Charlie, I wasn't ready to really honor myself within a relationship. I see that now. Perhaps Michael's back pocket has not been a terrible place to hide my heart while I've done some inner work.

Am I ready now? I don't know. But I am aware—first I must stop diving.

Downward Dog

There is no heat in my bedroom.

I don't mean that metaphorically, though sadly it does play in that context as well. I mean it quite literally. I live in a converted summer cottage and there is no heat on the second floor. There is only what rises up through the stairwell.

When my girls are home, we all sleep with our bedroom doors open to circulate the heat (and so I can hear them if they need me). Inevitably they both end up in my bed, along with the cat, who likes to perform opera from atop my headboard at about 3:00 a.m. (He really knows how to commit).

On the weekends, I close the bedroom door to avoid Diesel's pre-dawn serenade in the hopes of achieving that coveted and elusive deep sleep—and to save on heat. It seems silly to keep it cranking from downstairs just for my benefit. On cold nights, I just throw an extra comforter or two onto my bed.

I woke up this morning with a sense of the chill in the room, although I wasn't feeling it under all of the layers—flannel sheets, a quilt and two down comforters ... oh, and I may have slept in a sweater (I know, I know. *So* much sexiness). I was like a reverse Princess and the Pea. Waking up under the weight and warmth of these layers, it was hard to get out of bed. I loved the feeling of being cocooned, protected. I thought of those weighted blankets they sell for children with anxiety. The weight has a soothing quality.

Finally, I drag myself up, pad downstairs for some coffee—and admit, once again, that I am struggling. There is a pattern. The weekends can be hard for me. I don't have my children here, and I don't have to be at work. These are the two arenas in which I feel my strongest sense of self. They ground me.

I know that my parent-friends whose children are with them all the time may not be able to relate to "time off" from their kids as evoking a feeling of loss. When I was with my children seven days a week (especially when I was a stay-at-home mom), having a Saturday without my kids was like a vacation—a *really amazing* vacation. I would be giddy over it. However, when the "alone time" happens almost every weekend, the celebratory mood fades.

I miss them. A lot.

When I'm depressed, having my children around helps. For one thing, I love them, and being with them brings me true happiness. (Well, most of the time!) I am also aware of how my moods affect them, so I keep myself as even-keeled as I can when they are with me.

Then, on the weekends, I let it all out—and I depress the shit out of my dog, instead.

The Nothing

Gratitude and depression are not mutually exclusive. This seems like an incredibly important point to emphasize.

Can we let that sink in? *Gratitude and depression are not mutually exclusive.*

On Saturday, I was at the lowest I have been in a while. I was talking with Monica, and she asked me, very sincerely, what depression looks like to me when I close my eyes. I described a black hole, one into which I was desperately trying not to be pulled. After a moment I realized it wasn't a hole at all—at least, not in the sense that a hole has a bottom, a top and walls. Instead, it feels like the opposite of something—like a void.

My mind flashed to a movie I watched recently with my girls. It was a favorite from my own childhood, based on the book, *The Neverending Story* by Michael Ende. In it, a beautiful world full of amazing places and creatures is threatened to be sucked up by "The Nothing." The Nothing isn't a who or a what. It is literally *nothing*, and it is swallowing everything in its path.

"That's what it feels like." I said. "It feels like The Nothing."

"Do you remember what The Nothing actually was?" she asked, pointedly.

"Yes! The Nothing was *the absence of imagination.*"

And there it was. I have begun to lose sight of what I imagine my future to be. I am not looking hopefully and enthusiastically toward it. I am still standing in the rubble of the life that has tumbled down around me, and I'm afraid to look forward.

And there is no hope without imagination.

So, this seems like a good place to start. To be brave enough to imagine the future. It isn't just about appreciating what I have, it's also about believing that there's beauty and happiness to come.

We Were Seeds

A friend shared a quote today from Feliciana Cacciapuoti-Mathew. *"Often we're so focused on blooming that we forget that we need to dig deep before we can plant in the first place. You do not have to fight the dirt when you are aware of its purpose."*

I felt as though I was reading the exact right thing at the exact right moment. (I love when that happens.) I may have even gasped when the words landed.

I want to move forward, with hope, toward a brighter future. I want to be un-stuck. But also ... it's as if my adrenal glands are screaming, "No more surprises! No more change! We are *exhausted.* Just ... *no!*"

This wisdom, it struck me perfectly. *There are moments for planting and there are moments for blooming ...*

Right now, I am finding my footing. I am doing some deep digging. This is where I need to be right now—doing the work, sowing the seeds.

In time, I will once again be ready to bloom.

The Spotlight

Writing has felt cathartic to me in my grieving process. I love—and hate—calling out my demons: Fear, Anxiety, Shame, Sadness. By saying, "I see you," and shining light upon them, I feel as though I have lessened their power. It doesn't change the fact that these feelings live within me, but calling them out allows me to take back some control.

It feels like calling out a bully.

At the same time, I don't like to keep the spotlight on them— on these bullies. They are a part of me, but *they are not me*. I am so much more. In fact, looking back at my forty-four years, the times I have been ensconced in these weighty emotions is but a blip. These feelings are very much a product of my experiences of late, and not predominantly what lives within me at my core. I know this to be the truth.

My path to healing begins with making peace with the parts of me I do not love. Calling out the bullies, and perhaps even thanking them for illuminating so many things. Next, I can show Fear, Anxiety, Shame, and Sadness that, while they may bask in the spotlight now and again, they have never been, nor will they ever be, the stars of the show.

A few cameos, perhaps. That's all I'll give them. It's my story, after all.

The Canary
Flies Home

It was Friday night. Mom and I had spent the day as we do each week—a few hours at the infusion center, followed by dinner together and an overnight. This scheduled time together, though for an entirely shitty reason, has become important to both of us. Oddly enough, she feels best on the day she receives the infusion.

Aunt Anne and Uncle Ed had planned to join us for dinner and a pre-birthday celebration for me. What I *didn't* know was that Lynette was going to surprise me by walking through the door. Once I processed this vision of her, standing before me, I burst into tears. Oh, I have missed her so much. I couldn't believe I was wrapping my arms around her. I felt as though if I let go of her, she might vanish.

She had flown across the country just to be at my birthday party. Yes, my birthday party. You see, I haven't been feeling very social lately. I have begged off on a lot of invitations. With my birthday coming up, I figured the only way to make certain I would follow through with a proper celebration was to throw myself a party.

And so, the next day, twenty-five of my favorites gathered with me at the Camp to celebrate. If ever there was an elixir for sadness, this was one. Ten loved ones spent the night, leaving gradually throughout the next morning. Once everyone left, I settled in front of the fire with a book. Alone, but not at all lonely.

What Is A Year?

This morning, my girls enthusiastically got up early to begin birthday preparations. By the time I had showered and joined them downstairs, they had made their own lunches, their own breakfasts, and had set out coffee and birthday gifts for me. They were so excited to celebrate their mom.

It doesn't get much better than that.

After I dropped them at the bus stop, I got together for breakfast with my friend, Sarah, and then went off to a spa for a mini-retreat. I spent this quiet time reflecting on the year, as one tends to do on birthdays.

Last year, I spent my birthday in New York City. I had won a trip—complete with train tickets, hotel accommodations, dinner at a five-star sushi restaurant, and amazing seats to *Saturday Night Live*. Can you even believe that? *And* I had finally garnered the attention and affection of Michael. I was convinced that forty-four was going to *kick ass*. And it did.

It kicked my ass.

Hard.

So here I am, embarking on another year, and I find myself having anxiety about it. Will it be a good year, or a bad year? Is a good year even possible under the circumstances? Then, I realized that whole train of thought is foolish. What is a year, after all? It's a collection of months, weeks, days, hours … moments. Yes, there were a lot of bad days this past year. In fact, I experienced my worst days thus far. However, I had many good days too, and throughout these three hundred and sixty-five days I'd be willing to bet I had thousands of moments that made me smile and laugh. Hundreds of moments that filled me with gratitude. Dozens of moments that I will remember fondly, forever.

Perhaps, rather than focusing on having a "great year," what I should be doing is continuing to notice all of the wonderful moments within the next twelve months—moments that will always amount to so much more than all of the bad days put together.

Happy Thursday

Tomorrow is Thanksgiving, or as my mother and I have decided to call it, "Thursday."

Today, I went to pick up the turkey I had ordered at the local market. When they placed it on the counter, it seemed so small. The reality is that the thing was eighteen pounds—not really small at all. But last year, when they brought out the bird I'd ordered and placed it on the counter, we cracked up laughing, the cashier and me. It was just freakishly, comically big. (It may actually have been an ostrich.)

This year, with fewer people and a better handle on portions, I had aimed smaller. Deliberate as it was, noticing the contrast between the two birds still managed to highlight for me the absences we are feeling this year. I felt a wave of sadness looking at this "little" bird.

Last year's Thanksgiving was my favorite, ever. We had it for the first time at the Camp. To me, it was a perfect day. My dad loved having it there as well, and knowing now that it was his very last Thanksgiving, I am so grateful that we were able to do it there. This year we are missing from our Thanksgiving (umm ... *Thursday*) feast, my dad, but also Lynette (who sadly has returned to San Diego) and Ryan and his family (because ... New Jersey). I started to feel bad about that—about the voids we will feel tomorrow—and frankly, about the elephant in the room (my mom's cancer) that will be joining us in their place. *Who invited him, anyway? Doesn't he know how small the freakin' turkey is this year?*

Then I stopped, and I reminded myself how incredibly lucky I am to have all of the people who *will* be there to spend the day with us. Many people dread having to spend time with their relatives over the holidays. Other people aren't able to be with the ones they love, and others still ... well, they just don't have anyone at all.

As I look around the dinner table tomorrow, I will inevitably feel sadness for our loss and for missing those who are spending their Thursday elsewhere. I will also remember how lucky I am to have so many I love—whether they are at my table this year or not.

Keeping It Real

It is Thanksgiving night, and I am *not* feeling full of thanks, quite frankly. As I expressed yesterday, I had every intention of holding space for sadness and gratitude, simultaneously. And I did—but, if I'm honest, sadness won out for me tonight.

After Dad died, my friend Paul wrote to me, "I was on a few committees and boards with your dad. He was the kind of man who was quiet and listened respectfully to what everyone else had to say. When he finally spoke, the room got quiet. Everyone wanted to hear his thoughts." That so perfectly described Dad. He spoke eloquently and from the heart.

Dad would always make a toast on special occasions. We would all stop and listen with rapt attention, and often tears of gratitude. Tonight, I tried to take over this task. I stood up to speak—and, despite my love of words, all I could muster was a barely audible, "We miss you."

I am so grateful for the family that was here with me tonight. I love them all so much. Still, I was sad. Our world has changed. Mom quietly slipped off to bed at seven. The rest of the crowd hung in for a bit, but overall, the mood was subdued. We all just wanted to get through it. And we did.

After everyone left, the girls and I snuggled in together and watched *Elf.* Of all things, that helped—a few laughs and their warm bodies huddled close to mine as I ran my fingers through Ruby's hair.

We will all be okay, but I think it is important to drop expectations this holiday season and to be okay with whatever feelings show up. It is all going to be a jumble of gratitude, pain, joy, love, anger … and whatever else forces its (welcome or unwelcome) way into the mix.

They are all real and valid. They should be honored as such.

Choose Your Own Adventure

"You should come with me," he said. "I just booked a flight this morning."

This was Eric on the phone a week ago, trying to convince me to book a last-minute flight with him to surprise Lynette for her birthday. In response, I burst into tears. Being spontaneous was not something I could do. Not right now. After all, I take Mom to chemo on Fridays. And I'd have to arrange for the girls to spend a couple of extra days with Charlie. And there was Louie: with his insatiable and unpredictable appetite, there is no way I can leave him anywhere but at the boarding place, and they'd *definitely* be full at this point. And I'd have to find coverage at work. And flights during Thanksgiving weekend would be insanely expensive. And, and, and …

It all seemed impossible, even irresponsible. Still, I said, "Let me think about it. I really want to say yes." That was true—I really wanted to go, to get away for a few days. The idea of surprising Lynette had me overcome with emotion. I knew it would mean the world to her to have both of us there to celebrate her big four-zero. She's in a new city three thousand miles from home—three thousand miles away from almost everyone she loves.

Then, everything seemed to fall into place. My mother doesn't need me to be the one to take her every week to her infusion, that's just pressure I have placed on myself. Taking her allows me to feel as though I am doing something in a situation in which I am entirely helpless. Many other people have offered to take her—something my mother quickly pointed out. The girls were all set to stay an extra couple of days with Charlie. The boarding place said they'd make room for Louie. I got coverage at work, and with mine and Eric's airline miles I got a $760 ticket for $8.11.

I was going to California. In a week.

This morning, I woke up at my mother's house with the girls, having spent the night there. I'm not going to lie—it only took a few minutes before my anxiety started to kick in. *What if something happens to me, and the girls and my mother don't have me to take care of them? What if something happens to them while I'm away?*

The more I lose—the more it is demonstrated to me that I have no control—the more anxiety shows up for me. Over the past couple of years, the lessons in loss and powerlessness have been intense. I wish I could say that I have been able to relax into this awareness that I am not in control. I wish I could just allow life to unfold around me and to observe it without the little voice that whispers in my ear, *What if, what if, what if?* (Or, perhaps I could train the voice to whisper in a more optimistic tone. That would help.)

If anything, life has taught me that the things that really knock the wind out of me are the things I never see coming—like the fact that my ex-husband is actually my ex-wife, or that the loved one I had dinner with the night before has collapsed and will never again wake up, or that cancer is growing inside someone I love—someone who looks and feels perfectly healthy.

You'd think by now I'd have been able to let go of the idea that I control the narrative—or frankly, that I have *any idea* what my story is even about.

Life is sort of like one of those "Choose Your Own Adventure" books, isn't it? I loved those as a kid. In each chapter you get to decide which way to go. You come to a dramatic situation, and you have to decide: will I stow away on the boat (turn to page 23), will

I continue on horseback with my guide (turn to page 45), or will I return to the center of town to search for the lost map (turn to page 76)? We get to choose which way to go, but we don't get to decide what will happen when we get there. All we can do is choose a direction and hope for the best.

I don't ever want to stop choosing my next adventure—certainly not because of fear, or anxiety, or lack of imagination. So, California, here we come.

And here's my favorite part of this particular adventure (in case you hadn't put this together yet). Lynette and I, our birthdays are six days apart. While Eric and I were planning this trip to surprise her for her birthday, she had already booked a flight home to surprise me for mine. She flew across the country to celebrate with me, and now we are doing the same thing for her.

This is true love. If you ask me, there is no greater reason to embark on adventure than that.

Like the Stars at Noon

Depression and grief have been frustrating emotions for me. They are hollowing, damp, and heavy emotions and being within them is hard in and of itself. But for me the hardest part has been knowing these emotions are not my true nature. I know the lightness of which I am capable.

As Peter Matthiessen wrote, *"Yet, that light is always present, like the stars at noon."*

Lately, Joy, a once fluent language, now comes to me in hazy spurts of words. It is still there within me; I've not lost it completely. Being around others who speak it fluently and regularly helps to bring it all back—certain people, places, smells, sights, and sounds help to open the floodgates of memory and move me down the road to reclaiming Joy as my default.

After all, it is my first language.

A Wreath of Gratitude

I have always been adamantly opposed to putting up a Christmas tree in November. This year, though, I really wanted to decorate for Christmas early. *Bring on the shine and the joy!*

The girls and I went and picked out a tree. As a single woman, lugging the tree off of the top of my car and carrying it into the house myself brings me some perverse satisfaction. It's really not that hard to do, but it is one of those things, like using the grill and taking out the trash, that somehow always fell into the category of "manly jobs" during my marriage (though that does hold some irony now).

We put the tree up yesterday, and decorated it today. When it came time to get the decorations out, I found myself holding my breath a bit. Dad collapsed just two days after Christmas last year. It's hard not to muddy that stress and sadness together with the sights and sounds of Christmas.

As the girls and I began to sort through the decorations and ornaments, I couldn't find the massive tangle of Christmas lights. Every year I pull them out and curse myself for not having a better system for removing and storing them. They look like a massive squirrel's nest and it takes me forever to detangle them.

"That's weird," I thought out loud. "No lights? What could I have done with them?" I racked my brain to try to remember where I could have put them. Finally, Ruby pulled out a compact, perfectly spooled wreath of Christmas lights.

How the hell did that happen?

And then it hit me: it was Lynette. One night in early January, while I was sleeping in the ICU with dad, Lynette took down Christmas for me. Without a word, she put away all the decorations. She took down the tree. And she rolled my Christmas lights into a perfect wreath.

We are never alone, my girls and I. We have amazing people who love us. People who take care of us without being asked and in ways we have never even considered.

No Words

Chemotherapy is the oddest thing. My mother didn't feel the slightest bit sick until they started trying to cure her—until they started pumping her with poison to make her well. I spend time with her almost every day, but sometimes (more and more often), I don't know what to say. Everything I say seems wrong.

If I am happily talking about things I've done or plans I've made, that feels wrong. She isn't getting out much these days. She certainly isn't planning trips or buying concert tickets.

When I find myself complaining about my ordinary, day-to-day woes, their triviality hits me. My problems are small. *I* suddenly feel small. Insignificant. Useless.

Often, I just sit quietly. I listen. And I remember that showing up is much more important than finding the right thing to say. Nothing feels right at the moment, and no words will make it so.

Perhaps "I love you" can be heard the loudest when it's quiet.

How We Got Here

Two summers ago, I had a routine mammogram. Shortly afterward, I received a letter from the hospital stating that, while nothing had come up on the images, because of my "dense breasts" they could not guarantee that the screening was effective. They suggested I contact a Breast Health Center for more screening options.

I had received this same letter after previous mammograms. I remember having mentioned it to my mother on one occasion. She had said, with the dismissive brush of her hand, "Oh yeah. I get that letter every time, too. I think it's pretty standard."

Hmm.

I never took this suggestion for a follow-up seriously, even though my mother had already had breast cancer at age fifty-two. I don't know whether I was afraid or if I had just convinced myself it would never happen to me.

This time, for whatever reason, I followed up. After talking with the breast health specialist, I filled out a questionnaire—*did anyone in my family have cancer? How old was I when I had my first child? How long did I breastfeed? At what age did I begin menstruating?* (All of these things are relevant, apparently). Afterward, she informed me that, based on my answers I have a higher-than-average risk of developing breast cancer. That, coupled with my "hard-to-read" breasts (the nerve!), meant they wanted to alternate screenings— MRI and Mammogram—every six months.

It was almost an afterthought to mention that my mother's cousin's daughters had all tested positive for the BRCA mutation, an abnormality which correlates with a high rate of breast and ovarian cancer. One of them had passed away in her twenties. Two others had opted for dual prophylactic mastectomies. I have never met any of these women. I don't believe my mother has met them, either. This was just a story she told me once, in passing.

But as soon as I said *BRCA*, the doctor's demeanor changed. She strongly encouraged me to bring my mother in for genetic testing. The first available appointment was several months out. I decided that I would wait until it got closer to tell my mother about it. I didn't want her to worry.

In the meantime, some very stressful things happened in my family. I knew my parents were worried about me. Not wanting to add more stress, I rescheduled the appointment for a few months later, never having told her about it to begin with.

Then, Dad died, and I rescheduled again. At this point it had been almost a year since my initial appointment, and I knew we *had* to go, no matter what was going on. And we did. My mother had the genetic screening done, which was a simple blood test. They tested her (and not me yet) because if I had it, I would have gotten it from her. Therefore, if she was negative, I wouldn't need the test. If she was positive, her siblings and children would all benefit from a test. We waited three long weeks for the results, and sure enough, she was positive. She has the mutation. They immediately started talking about more aggressive screenings and other preventative measures, and then they tested me.

Three more weeks I waited for my own test results, vacillating daily (hourly?) between being sure I *must* be negative (because the Universe couldn't possibly hate me this much), and planning for the certain removal of my ovaries and breasts (because the Universe definitely hates me this much). I had already decided I was not going to mess around in the event of a positive finding. A 72% chance of developing breast cancer—as opposed to 12% in the general population, and 47% percent chance of ovarian cancer? No, thank you.

Lop these things off. They've never been particularly noteworthy to begin with ... and they're "dense" to boot!

In the end, my test came back negative. To say I was relieved is an understatement. Now to support my mother through her recommended preemptive measures. They highly recommended the removal of her ovaries, because there is no effective screening for ovarian cancer (that is why the outcomes are often so poor. By the time a woman feels sick, it is often too late). We were ready to nip this in the bud.

It never occurred to me that my mother was already sick.

The MRI showed three tumors. The largest one was hidden under scar tissue from her breast cancer surgery twenty years ago. Two others were too small to have been detected by mammogram.

I'll be honest, I was really angry about a few things: Why was she never tested for BRCA? I understand they didn't know about this gene twenty years ago. But in the years since, no one has suggested this test to her as a breast cancer survivor?

And then, the self-blame. Why had I rescheduled this genetic appointment *twice?* How much better would her prognosis have been, had we discovered this a year ago?

And also—*what the ever-loving fuck!* Was this seriously happening? *Now?*

I know we can't go down the rabbit hole of *what ifs.* It is an absolute blessing that I followed up on my goddamn dense breasts when I did. Otherwise, my mom never would have been tested. She would not have had the MRI that caught the tumor. By the time she felt sick, it might have been too late. I can't beat myself up for not following through sooner—but I know it'll haunt me forever if she doesn't survive this.

Just Like People

I used to spend a lot of time picking out the perfect Christmas tree. I'd wander around in the cold, agonizing over each one—its height, its symmetry. I did not take this decision lightly.

Eventually, my children began to weigh in on the selection process. Their criteria weren't quite as ... *clear* as mine. It is hard to let go of being in charge of tree selection, but when my children declare their undying love for a tree, its imperfections lose their significance. And what I ultimately realized was this: every single tree is beautiful when it is dressed in light and love.

Just like people.

Serenity Now!

I had a really wonderful weekend. I'd even say it was perfect. My girls were home with me for the first weekend in what seemed like forever. On Saturday, we lounged around all day as the snow fell. I hate to brag, but both days I made us a breakfast that didn't pop up out of the toaster.

Saturday night, we had friends over for dinner—the kind of friends who are easy and relaxed company. We puttered around again on Sunday morning and went to a matinée in the afternoon. We simply enjoyed each other's company. It was fun and cozy, simple and relaxed.

Which is why my anxiety today was a real kick in the pants. There it was, tapping me on the shoulder this morning as soon as I left the bus stop. I knew I had a hard conversation ahead of me with one of my employees, and I knew she was going to feel hurt. (There's nothing I hate more than hurting someone, except maybe pretending a conversation isn't necessary when it is.) I worried about it all day. I felt distracted and anxious. My chest ached, and my hands shook.

But I also noticed something interesting. In the past, when anxiety has gripped me, I've felt as though I was trapped in my body, experiencing a horrible, inescapable sensation. I have wanted to unzip my own skin and step out of it.

Today, after a while, I was able to recognize the feeling and pull away from it. It was as though I had a bird's-eye view of myself. I could see myself struggling, but it didn't feel quite as awful, because

I knew I just needed to ride it out. Watching from my perch above myself, I could see my anxiety *was not me*, but rather something I was experiencing in that moment.

As soon as the girls and I got home and settled in, I knew enough to tell them that I'd had a stressful day and needed to wind down a bit. I started a hot bath and poured myself some herbal tea (if herbal tea were red and made from grapes). I dumped about a half a bottle of lavender oil into the tub. I lit some candles and turned out the lights. As I lay there in the candlelight, steeping in a warm lavender bath and listening to some clinky, clanky meditation music with wine in hand, I started to let go of the day.

Yes, I'm alone with the bath, the wine, the candlelight, the clinky-clanky music ... and my incomplete Christmas list and the appointment I forgot to make and the list of things I have to accomplish at work this week and the worry that I've offended a friend and the really kind text message I forgot to respond to and a critical replay of the hard conversation I had earlier ...

In the words of Frank Costanza, "SERENITY NOW!"

I worked at bringing my focus back to the desire to relax and let it all go. Finally, as the tub began to feel tepid, I felt my blood pressure drop. I felt my muscles relax. I could breathe easier.

I pulled myself from the tub just as it began to grow cold. Feeling restored, I was ready to help with homework, play Parcheesi, and make dinner.

Fancy Christmas Anxiety

The holiday season is a time of love and giving—and also, for many of us, a time of heightened anxiety and stress. I always worry during this time of year that I have forgotten to do something or to buy something. That, somehow, I am going to leave someone I care about feeling overlooked or disappointed.

I was thinking the other day: how do people with more than two children remember all of the things they need to do at this time of year? Yes, there's the shopping to be done for the kids—but also for their teachers, their coaches (all very deserving of our gratitude!), and then, of course, there are the special events. How do you manage when it's more than one school? Kudos to them all. Really.

I have struggled all year with memory and organizational issues. So, coming into a time of year when there is so much more to do and to remember, this quote I saw online struck me particularly funny: *"It's time to trade in my regular anxiety for my fancy Christmas anxiety!"*

The logical thing to do is to back off a bit where I can, to not voluntarily add more things to my "to-do" list. The dilemma with which I am faced is this: adding things to my plate can cause anxiety, but *doing things for other people* helps me to combat depression. It's the classic uppers vs. downers dilemma.

It isn't much of a dilemma, actually. If my anxiety is presently caused by worrying about the amount of love and joy I am spreading in the world, that's a pretty good kind of anxiety to have, right? The fancy Christmas kind?

But here's the painful truth—I see The Nothing ahead of me, that big black fog of darkness I will have to walk through at the other side of Christmas. The night of December 26th was the last time I saw my dad conscious. It was the last time I felt his arms around me. It was the last time I heard him say, "I love you."

So … I know exactly what I'm doing with all of this "doing" for everyone else. I am begging the question, *If I create as much light as I can between now and then, can I hold it off?*

Can my light push away The Nothing?

Show Them

The worst thing I can think of to say about my father is that he was sometimes absentminded. I'd realize halfway through a story that he hadn't heard a word I'd said. Somehow this was endearing—this habit of wandering off in his own thoughts. To me, he was perfect. Perfectly imperfect. My point is—he was easy to love.

I know it is easy for me to sit here and tell you to appreciate everyone you love, even the ones who are hard to love sometimes. But I am going to do it anyway. Nothing brings into focus the unpredictability and fragility of our time with one another more than death. (I know, I'm being an Oracle of the Obvious here, but it's true).

At this point in my life, it makes me feel great pain to see people who love each other construct roadblocks to the giving and receiving of that love. Whether it is out of fear, anger, a lack of understanding, or poor communication, it doesn't matter. When I would give anything to have back someone I've lost, it is incredibly hard to reconcile the idea that *anyone* would withhold their love. That *anyone* would choose to close their heart when the time to open it is not infinite. Time is not promised. If you love someone, say it—but don't stop there.

Show them.

Show them by opening your heart, your home.

Show them by having the hard conversations.

Show them by not being afraid of what you don't understand.

Show them by choosing to see the best in them.

Show them by loving them even when it's hard to do.

Show them by remembering why you began loving them in the first place.

Show them by giving them second chances, or third.

Show them by not giving up.

Show them while you can.

Show them.

Triage

This past week I have been thinking about the idea of triage—ranking injuries according to severity to determine which ones take priority.

We had about eight months to focus on tending to the wound my dad's death inflicted upon us all. He died in January. August was a turning point for me; I felt like my wound was healing. I had come to understand that it would never completely go away, but I didn't have to expend so much energy tending to it daily. It was no longer urgent care—it was maintenance.

Then came Mom's cancer diagnosis. Energy and attention shifted immediately to my mother. Strong as she is, chemo has been challenging for Mom. These last four months I have been more focused on how she is feeling physically than on how we are all feeling emotionally.

Nothing takes attention off of the death of a loved one more than the very visceral fear of losing another.

The mother-wound usurped the father-wound.

Mom finished a twelve-week course of chemo last week, so they gave her a week off before starting her next round. This means she will have a full week of feeling human. Just in time for Christmas. Just in time to fully experience the pain of our first Christmas without Dad. Just in time for his death-iversary.

And so, triage shifts again to the father-wound, busted open and in need of urgent care.

May I Sit at Your Table?

Yesterday afternoon I sat at the bar at a beautiful waterfront restaurant with Lynette and Ryan. There were some tears. We laughed at ourselves as we dabbed our eyes with cocktail napkins. I mean ... poor us, crying into our oysters and wine.

Maybe this is a big part of my struggle. That there is so much abundance around me—nourishment in all forms. Yet, the fact that I have the time, the money, and the wonderful family to indulge in an afternoon like this doesn't bring back my father. It doesn't make my mother less sick. It doesn't make life less heavy right now.

As soon as I got into my car alone, I really let go. Big, heaving sobs. I pulled myself together to run a few errands—to the grocery store, the liquor store, and the pharmacy, and to pick up one last gift. I pasted on a smile—but, oddly, I felt as though every clerk was treating me with kid gloves. They each were kind, but subdued, offering a particularly gentle "Happy Holidays."

When I got home and looked in the mirror, I understood. It would have been glaringly obvious to anyone who looked at me that I had been crying. In that moment, taking in my reflection, I felt guilty for having subjected the world to my obvious despair—*and on Christmas Eve–Eve.* How rude.

But there it is, isn't it?

There is this expectation of joy that we place upon the world at this time of year. None of us want to admit when we aren't feeling in the spirit. The truth is, we all have our ups and downs in this rollercoaster of life. When we're at a highpoint at Christmastime, it is an insanely intoxicating time of year, full of joy and hope. When we are at a low point, we become a detached witness to the joyful hustle and bustle. We don't feel a part of it, and that makes us feel all kinds of shitty emotions—ungrateful, guilty, embarrassed. Like we don't belong. Like we're at a party we weren't invited to. It is that feeling of being lonely in a crowd—of searching the room for our people—the really-I-am-so-blessed-and-grateful-but-I-am-also-really-sad-and-this-is-not-my-most-wonderful-time-of-the-year people.

Ahh ... there you are. May I sit at your table? I'll bring oysters and wine ... and lots of cocktail napkins.

The Truth

The other day I went into a bit of a tailspin, worried over the idea that I may have offended someone I care about. It was silly, really, but boy did I get whipped up. I realized later that while the idea that I may have hurt his feelings worried me, it was the worry that he wasn't going to be honest about it that caused even greater dis-ease within me.

That he would be upset and pretend he wasn't.

That he would be someone he's not.

Honesty and transparency have become like air to me. I choke and struggle and gasp if I feel I am being deprived of them—by others, and from within myself.

That is why I am here, telling you.

It Isn't the Dying That Matters

We have come upon the one-year anniversary of Dad's death. Mom wanted to have a dinner out in honor of him. As we sat together at the restaurant, I thought about how hard it is to comprehend that someone so unassuming and humble could have left such a big void at the dinner table. Our collective aching for his presence was as tangible as the cocktails we hoped would numb it.

Throughout the day I kept replaying what I was doing one year prior. I'd spent the day roller skating with friends and family, followed by a spaghetti dinner with the girls and their two buddies. The five of us sat down to watch *The Princess Bride*. It is eerie to recall what a fun day it had been—before the call.

I will never forget that call. When I think of it, it raises my heart rate. I feel my chest constrict. Sometimes it nearly brings me to my knees, still—recalling Ryan's voice on the other end of the phone. I knew it was him (caller ID), but his voice was contorted by the most gut-wrenching chords of despair and pleading, *"What's wrong with Dad?"*

I knew nothing. I hadn't been told yet. For a moment we took comfort that it must be a mistake. How could I not know our lives had changed? Moments later we learned the truth and I was frantic to get to the hospital. *What if he dies, and I don't get there in time?* Little did I know I would have a week of purgatory to live through before kissing his warm cheek for the last time.

I have thought a lot about death and what I'd wish for Dad's passing if I'd gotten to choose. Would I wish for a sudden death, so we wouldn't have had the agony of hope? An extended illness, so we'd have had more time to prepare? Or would I have chosen the slow acceptance with which most of us were faced that last week—the week in which Dad's heart, in the cruelest betrayal, continued to fuel his body but not his brain?

After much deliberation, I've decided it is all utter shit. All of it. There's no good way to lose a loved one. There's no perfect scenario that is going to mitigate the shattering of your heart.

But, my dear, it isn't the dying that matters. *It's the living.*

Calendar

Perhaps a bit too eagerly, I pulled the 2017 calendar off of the wall and threw it into the recycling bin. Good riddance.

A few minutes later, I circled back into the kitchen and fished it back out again. For whatever reason, I had to take one last look at it—at this terrible train wreck of a year that began with a death and ended with a fight for life.

Before I could relegate that collection of pages to be recycled—to literally becoming something else entirely—I needed to see it one more time. My year in review.

Bracing myself, I opened up the calendar to January, and to my surprise I found a completely blank page. February was blank as well. It was as if time stood still for those two months—as if nothing happened, or nothing that happened mattered.

The living resumed in March, and from the looks of it I made sure I lived. Yes, there were doctor's appointments, school obligations, and other such reminders, but also ... I flew to Georgia, Virginia, Florida, and California. I saw two theatre productions. I saw some fabulous live bands perform, as well as two comedians. I took two trips to Maine, including our infamous island adventure. I visited Cape May, New Jersey with my mother for the first time in many years. I spent more days than I ever have, during one year, at my favorite place—the Camp. I celebrated the fiftieth wedding anniversary of two of my favorite people. Twice, I looked on as people I love vowed to love one another in sickness and in health. I hosted two festivals at my school. I took my faculty out for a holiday dinner. I threw myself a birthday party.

These are the events of which I was reminded as I flipped through the pages. So many good memories of happy moments, events, or days—all sprinkled throughout an incredibly challenging year.

However, these events scrawled throughout the calendar aren't really what I'd like to take away from my review of the year. What isn't written there in rainbow Sharpie markers is all that I learned. I learned so much—about myself especially, but also about others. Tragedies, and what happens in their midst and in their wake, are illuminating in so many ways.

I learned that emotion and self-expression are not indicative of weakness. Nothing requires such a summoning of strength as does complete vulnerability and honesty. To say "Here I am!" and then voice what is really on my mind and in my heart—that is incredibly brave. I learned not to be afraid to share from the deepest parts of me, because that is where we truly connect as human beings. We all have these dark and tender places within us.

You'll laugh when I tell you that this year is wrapping itself up nicely for me with the flu virus this New Year's Eve. Oh, you sweetheart of a year—I wouldn't expect anything less from you. But just know that *you didn't beat me.* All you did was show me that I can handle more than I ever imagined.

Which leads me to my greatest accomplishment of this year:
I kept showing up, every day.

When We're Ready

On the first day of the calendar year, we all get a clean slate—a chance to offer the world a new us. A chance to hit the reset button, and to begin a new chapter of our lives.

I'm sorry, but that is a *lot* of pressure to put on one day.

What if, at the stroke of midnight, you find yourself in a state that feels opposite of optimism and renewal? What if you are not in a position to have a fresh start, but rather, are right in the middle of a very challenging period of your life—something beyond your ability to "reset?"

Case in point: last year I rang in the new year curled up on a reclining chair in the ICU. Rather than fireworks and cheers, I laid there listening to the beeping of the IV drip, and the hum of the respirator, which (as it turned out) would only keep my father alive for five more days. On New Year's Day, my sister-in-law, Karen, remembers being in the room when someone from maintenance came in with a power tool and removed the calendar from the wall, replacing it with a fresh, shiny new one. The perversity seared it into her memory. *Happy New Year!*

As the clock strikes midnight this year, I find myself thinking about Karen, who lost her own father just a few days ago. We know all too well how this year will be for her family. Meanwhile, Melissa ushered in the new year from Jaime's bedside in the ICU. Meanwhile, another friend is faced with an impending divorce—a divorce that he really does not want. Meanwhile, Charlie is struggling to be understood and accepted by some members of her own family.

And meanwhile, for us Harveys … with luck, Mom has two more months of intense chemo, then surgery, before we can hope to see her good health return.

My point is, many people are enduring hard things—things for which there is presently no reset button. To many, the words "Happy New Year" will ring hollow.

But the good news—to my thinking, anyway—is that January 1 is a completely arbitrary date to have been chosen as the first day of the year. A year is a circle, isn't it? (Well, technically it's an ellipse. It is a rotation around the sun.) There is no stopping nor starting point. We all go round and round.

So, how about we take the pressure off of those who might be feeling robbed of their fresh start as of midnight on this totally random point in the Earth's orbit? Because we can have a fresh start any old time we choose. In fact, we have the possibility of one every single day. Whenever we're ready.

I've Gotta Go,
I Love You

They kept my dad heavily sedated during his nine days in the hospital. (Can you believe they can sedate someone who is already unconscious? Oh, the things you learn!). They had to do this because he was having seizures constantly—petit mal, the kind you can't see. The doctor described them as electrical storms in his brain. They didn't want the storms to (further) damage his brain, so they sedated him to stop them. The problem was, with the heavy sedation, they couldn't tell whether there was any "normal" brain function. So, we had to wait, and wait. They'd cut back the sedatives and the storms would begin again—so they'd put him back on the drugs, again and again.

The entire week—this week, last year—we were in this horrifying purgatory. We are all having flashbacks. Both of my brothers have called me today. I talked with each of them only for a few minutes, as I was at work. At a certain point in each conversation, someone at work needed my attention and I said, "I've gotta go. I love you," when what I wanted to say was ...

I know. I'm here too. I'm right here with you. I'm here, watching my tears drip onto his impossibly warm hand. I'm here, our hearts soaring at the sight of his suddenly open eyes, only to realize they see nothing. I'm here, sitting with you on the cold floor in the corridor, because somehow it is less depressing than the waiting room. I'm here, sitting in the hospital chapel, embarrassed by the fact that my first real talk with God is happening here, in a glorified closet—after all of the hallowed places I've been. I'm here, in the cold conference room with too many chairs, waiting to hear them say what we already know. I'm here, wanting to throttle the neurologist with the nervous habit of smirking while she says the worst things a person can hear.

I'm here, but I also have to be *here*—today. Life goes on, despite the storms in my brain.

Dad, I've gotta go. I love you.

The Hole

I have a handful of loved ones going through really hard things right now. Each situation is, in a sense, completely different from that of the others. However, a common thread exists—and that is that none of us pictured ourselves here, experiencing this moment. We are all dealing with things we never expected we would. Things were not supposed to be this way.

That's the hardest part to get our heads around, isn't it? Reconciling what we thought would happen with what has happened or what is happening. We all have ideas of how our lives will be—our careers, our loves, our families, and our health.

Maybe things haven't fallen into place for us. Or maybe they have—only they've slipped away slowly, in tiny increments, or so suddenly it has taken the wind right out of us. A friend wrote to me that he "fell through a hole he never knew was there." How many of us have experienced this moment—when, suddenly, our legs have come out from under us, and we find ourselves in a free fall? I bet most of us have experienced this to varying degrees—or, should I say, to varying depths.

As you know, there have been a lot of surprises in my life over the past few years. These happenings have loosened my attachment to the idea that things will follow a predictable course. I think I have gotten better about not having expectations—or at least never imagining I know what will happen next.

Here's what I know for sure. When life is moving along beautifully, it will change. When life is really hard, it will change. The pace of these changes may happen too fast or too slow for our liking—but things will always change.

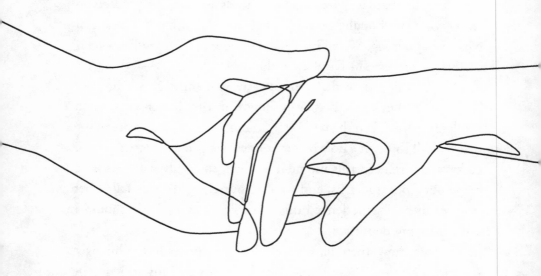

The Recliner

My mother has impeccable taste, both in her home and on her person. Owning a reclining chair was, for many years, tantamount to wearing sweatpants. It's just something she would never do. I'm not really sure how the (very tasteful) recliner ended up in my parents' den, but I imagine it had something to do with my mother having loved my father enough to agree to own it—as long as it was to remain in the back room, where no one else would see it.

When I went to visit her yesterday and found her in this recliner, wrapped in a blanket like a small child, the image threw me—how far she appeared to be from herself. From the strong, non-sweat-pant wearing, ever-moving, recliner-loathing woman that she is. She seemed so small. My mother is only about 5'2" so, to be fair, she *is* small, but her presence—a walking contradiction of grace and will—to me, is always large.

She's had a cold this week, on top off some ass-kicking (and hopefully cancer-kicking) chemo. This path to wellness is not an easy one, and I can't help but think how hard it has been for her, having had only eight months to adjust to being a widow before having to adjust to being a widow with cancer. Life can be cruel. Still, she'll smile and say, "We had a good run"—as if all of those years of happiness were the result of a bargain she'd made with the devil and now she's just paying her dues.

There are bound to be many more days in the recliner (and maybe even some days in sweatpants, you never know) before she rids herself of these tumors—these very rude and unwelcome new roommates. But she will prevail. I know she will.

Today when I walked into the house just before 8:00 a.m., she was up and ready to cross some things off of her to-do list before she gets whacked with chemo again tomorrow. I am not sure whether she got to those things, but I was encouraged that she was thinking about it.

Mom has always hated winter. I imagine she would prefer to just sleep through these next few months—to hibernate, and wake up in the spring like one of her daffodil bulbs. To wake up on the other side of this, when that garden that she has so lovingly planted and carefully tended all these years comes back into bloom, and so does she.

Return of the Light

How do we keep opening our hearts and being vulnerable when people—and life—can be so unpredictable? How do we remain inspired to plan for the future when so much is beyond our control? As I was emerging from the shower (I get a lot of good thinking done in there) it occurred to me that the answer to both questions is the same. Optimism.

The unexpected *is* to be expected, so we cannot fixate on things following a predictable course—on them following our plan. We must learn to go with the flow, adjust, and bend to sometimes fall apart and then piece ourselves back together again.

That is a good thing to understand, theoretically, but when life throws a lot of surprises at us over a short period of time, we may become exhausted. We may also become apathetic. Isn't it easier not to try? Not to care? Not to plan?

I used to feel full of optimism. I was inspired—by family, by work, by love, and by *life*. But the events of the last year or so have left me so exhausted that I have ceased to feel that optimism. I have lost it. And I want it back.

We are presently living through the darkest days of the year, but each day brings us more and more light—more and more lightness. I don't want to spend so much time fighting off the darkness that I cease to notice the light.

The Bucket

The other day online I came across a video titled *Why Depression is All in Your Head.*

I hit the volume button to hear what she had to say—this young and perky blonde. I was prepared to be annoyed. After all, for quite some time now I have been advocating for people's right to feel their feelings—depression, anger, grief, anxiety, all of it. Not to mention the fact that the title was invalidating to so many people who are going through very real struggles.

There was nothing particularly new or surprising—stop talking about being depressed all the time, eat well, exercise, get fresh air, smile, compliment people, and get sleep. Still, as I sat there and listened to her, I had to admit she had some valid points.

Maybe I wasn't as annoyed as I thought I would be because I was ready to hear it. I am ready to shed this heaviness. I think I already have, to an extent. There's this piece of me that feels like I am supposed to stay down in the well until my mother beats cancer, until her treatments and surgeries are over. How can I feel happiness when she is struggling?

Then I realized—I am more capable of helping her out of the well if I'm not in it, too. If we're both down here, we're kind of screwed, aren't we?

Lady of the Labyrinth

You'd think I'd know by now that this is not a linear journey. Sometimes I feel so confident that I am heading in the right direction, only to find myself once again lost in emotion. When this happens, I feel disoriented, frustrated, and even a bit embarrassed.

Life can be confusing sometimes. Other times the answers seem so obvious. The problem is that when life becomes hard and confusing, we often forget what those obvious answers were, and we become lost. It's really all a big maze, isn't it? Life is a labyrinth.

Sometimes the way out seems very clear. We begin to gleefully run in what we believe to be the right direction. Other times, we come up against barriers and walls, and think to ourselves, *Wait, haven't I been here before? This looks familiar. Umm ... did I just go in a circle* again?

Yes, we have—and yes, we did. Often, we come up against the same barriers again and again, and we have to remember how it was that we escaped the last time, and the time before that, and the time before that.

Or, maybe, we try a new path.

There is no way out, for the labyrinth is of our own making—and as such it is ever-changing, ever-evolving, ever-*teaching*. We will never be free until we cease to be.

Sometimes I think that I would like to reach a place in life where I can meet everything with an even keel—to keep my composure whether faced with a clear path or a wall before me. But then I think: I actually *like* being a person who feels deeply. I wouldn't want to give up my highs in order to not feel the lows. I'd rather feel lost and frustrated at times if it means I get to feel the exhilaration of those moments when the path seems so clear. Surviving the difficult days is what makes the blissful ones ... well, blissful.

Perhaps it's all about getting to a place wherein the clear paths and the obstacles are met, not necessarily with the same emotional response, but with the same respect. Each one is a teacher. They are all part of the human experience, here in the labyrinth of life.

Worthy

Have you ever noticed how hard it is for most of us to accept praise, compliments ... anything flattering? I wonder—when does that start to happen? Young children love to be complimented. They beam. Their posture straightens. They feel worthy.

You have really gotten good at pumping on the swings!

You're right, I have! I am a great pumper!

Something happens to many of us along the way. We stop believing the good things about ourselves—or, at least, it becomes much harder to believe them. Sometimes, we don't even hear the good things being said; we tune them out, subconsciously dismissing them. Sometimes, we hear them, but we just don't believe them to be true. Sometimes, we even try to talk others out of a compliment!

Oh no, not me. Oh, that wasn't a big deal. Oh, no, so-and-so is much better ...

I am blessed with very expressive children. Sometimes, they'll say to me, "Mom, you are the best mom *in the world.*" In the past, I have really had to work to resist the urge to say, "Oh, that's not true. You simply don't have a frame of reference. I'm the only mom you've ever had! I am *definitely not* the best mom in the world. Far from it!"

In my head, I'd run through all of my shortcomings as a mother. I'd stop myself just short of worrying that they might have Stockholm Syndrome. Finally, I realized that by doing this (even just quietly in my head), I am missing the point, which is that, to them, I *am* the best they can imagine. Isn't that incredible?

So, I have learned to simply say, "Thank you!" and to savor these proclamations. Especially because I know, as they enter their teenage years, I am not likely to be placed so firmly upon a pedestal.

I am also getting better at accepting the nice things other people say to me, too. I now say "Thank you" when people compliment me. (Revolutionary, I know!) But I still notice it, this predisposition to hear the criticism so much more loudly than the compliments.

A friend wrote to me the other night, expressing some really kind things. "You are an inspiration," he wrote. *What?* Never have I been called that. What a beautiful thing to say. And I initially skipped right over it, along with all the other nice things he expressed. Instead, I focused on taking a gentle suggestion he made and turning it into a criticism. Somehow that was easier to accept as the predominant point of the message than its true intention, which was one of encouragement and love. It wasn't until later that his words flashed back to me. I went back to re-read the message ... and I allowed myself to feel worthy of his words.

Fuck That

I knew my mother was feeling better when she sweetly suggested I put a sign outside her door telling the priest making rounds to *Fuck Off.* I howled with laughter. Understand, this is a woman who didn't give herself permission to curse in front of me until I was about forty years old. I still find her use of the word "fuck" entirely surprising—and therefore, absolutely hilarious.

She doesn't have anything against priests, per se. After all, one of her favorite people was her cousin Shawn, a Catholic priest. I think it's just that—well, sometimes grief brings people closer to God, their faith, their church, and sometimes it simply makes people say, "WTF? Screw you for letting this happen." At the moment, Mom finds herself in the latter camp. Within eight months she lost the man she'd loved since she was fifteen years old and found out she has stage three breast cancer. Personally, I think "WTF" is a perfectly justifiable reaction.

So, when the priest started lurking in the hall outside hospital room 223 (where she had ended up after some complications of chemotherapy), it really was in his best interest to steer clear. I told him she was resting, because ... well, I like to keep my options open.

This is where I tell you Mom is fine. Well, she's *okay*—as good as can be expected, anyway. She will be discharged today. It was scary seeing her so sick—sick enough for me to drive her to the emergency room at 4:00 a.m.

Seeing her so small and vulnerable in the hospital bed, I was thinking about the time I spiked a high fever—the highest fever I can remember. Beau was only a month old. I didn't know what to do. Charlie was out of town. I felt too sick to care for my own baby. I was worried that the very milk she needed to sustain her would make her sick. I called my mother at 5:00 a.m. She rushed over. She took care of Beau, and she took care of me.

There was no discussion about it.

It just was.

These past few days, I felt a flipping of roles as mother became daughter, daughter became mother. She has always taken care of me; I will now take care of her.

There is no discussion about it.

It just is.

She is such a fighter. I feel a bit in awe of her. This morning, when I arrived at the hospital with coffee, she was up, showered, dressed, and ready to go. Unfortunately, they decided she needed to have a blood transfusion before they would release her.

"Well Mom," I said, "I think you're going to have to put the Johnny back on."

"Fuck that," she said with a smirk.

Shamefaced

I was trying to figure out if what I was feeling would be defined as shame or as guilt. So, I looked up their definitions and there it was—*"shamefaced."* That was just too good a word to pass up.

Sometimes I feel shamefaced, and for all the wrong reasons. I intend to stop.

I have a lot on my plate. Most of us do. As the mother of two young girls, as the daughter of a newly widowed, cancer-fighting mother, as a small business owner responsible for the livelihoods of a dozen amazing women and the care of many precious children, and for maintaining the confidence of over a hundred parents who leave us their world each morning ... I care. I care *so deeply* about all of it—about everyone. I feel so grateful and proud to be given this privilege.

And ... it's a lot.

It's a whole lot of caring about very important people and very important things. So why, in light of all this caring, do I feel "shamefaced" when it comes to caring for myself?

I have a confession to make. Every day for the past week, despite the many things on my plate, I have either taken a long walk (in the woods or at the beach), or I have gone to yoga. Each of these things take about an hour and a half. An hour and a half. And every time I take this time to care for myself, it feels like *the most decadent thing I could possibly do.*

I know this is what I need in order to maintain my sanity. I know that it is, in the end, in the best interest of *every other human who needs something from me*. And yet, this morning after I got up, made breakfasts and lunches for my kids, fed the dog, drove the kids to the bus, cleaned the kitchen, took out the trash, started some laundry, spent an hour and a half doing tax prep and responding to emails, I *still* felt shamefaced about going to yoga. About taking that little bit of time before ramping back up to do *all the things* for the rest of the day and evening.

I texted my colleague, Stacy, at work and said I would be "out of touch" for an hour. I almost lied and said I had "an appointment." I am not a liar—and yet, I felt like I should lie. Because it felt like I was disrespecting her, as she was still hard at work and I was doing this thing *just for me*.

This is so messed up.

Whether your stolen moments of sanity look like finding a quiet corner of the house to enjoy a cup of tea or a glass of wine, or a phone call to a friend, or a walk with your dog, or a yoga class … whatever your self-care time looks like, can we just acknowledge how hard it is to take that time without feeling like we should be doing something else—probably for *someone* else?

Why is it so hard to learn to put on our own oxygen masks before assisting others?

So many of us mistakenly wear our selflessness as a badge of honor. *Look at all I do for everyone else all day long! No, nothing for me!* We should be proud of all that we do for others—absolutely. We should be proud of our ability and our willingness to recognize all that needs doing, and doing it.

And we should also be adept at identifying our own needs and tending to those. We should, perhaps, be even prouder of that.

One-Couches and
Sugar-Muffins

This morning, I was making pancakes when Beau sidled up next to me. Taking her cue from me, she grabbed a pancake in her hand and began eating it as she leaned up against the counter.

"Mmm. This takes like a sugar-muffin," she said.

"A sugar-muffin?" I asked.

"Yeah, you know the muffins that have frosting ... oh, whoops! I mean, a *cupcake*."

"Ah, yes. That *is* a sugar muffin!" I exclaimed, and we laughed.

"Remember the one-couch?" she asked, laughing still.

A couple of months ago we were looking for a couch. We came across a big leather chair, and sinking into it she said, "I think Papa would really have liked this one-couch."

"One-couch?"

"Yeah, *a couch for one*," she said, giving me the look that conveys, "*Duh* ..."

"Umm ... I think it's called a *chair?*"

"Oh. Yeah."

We had laughed hysterically.

"Sometimes my brain just doesn't work that well," she said now, still cramming pancake into her mouth.

"I think your brain works perfectly. You just see things differently than other people sometimes. If you ask me, *one-couch* and *sugar-muffin* are way better descriptors than *chair* and *cupcake*. You have the mind of a poet. That's a beautiful thing."

"Hmm, maybe. I guess I'll just sit in my one-couch and eat some sugar-muffins."

Fear Is A Needy
Neighbor

When you have dealt with fear a lot over a short period of time, there are some benefits—the biggest one being that it is no longer an unfamiliar sensation. You don't have to go through that, *"Oh shit, what is this feeling?"* inner dialogue. You know the feeling. And you usually understand why it is being revealed in a particular moment or circumstance.

My fear has become a bit like a needy neighbor with a penchant for pop-ins. Even though I didn't invite her over, it seems like the compassionate choice is to welcome her in—to see if I can ease her suffering in some way. Sometimes, that little bit of attention is all she needs. She feels seen, and she can then go off on her not-so-merry way. Other times, she camps out on my couch for so long I'm afraid she'll never leave—and boy, does she ramble on and on.

She doesn't seem to do this as much anymore—the camping out, that is. It helps that she doesn't need to keep reintroducing herself. That's a real time saver. I know her pretty well. And she's not *all* bad. She does usually bring wine and desserts with her, and she spurs some interesting self-reflection. She at least *tries* to be a good guest.

The other day this needy neighbor showed up unexpectedly (as she is wont to do). It seemed like she was making herself pretty comfortable on my couch. I grew quite bored with her chatter, and decided to distract myself with a book. I picked one up, flipped through the pages, and read this passage by Mark Nepo:

"When gripped by fear or anxiety, the reflex is to hold on, speed up, or remove oneself. Yet when we feel the reflex to hold on, that is usually the moment we need to let go. When we feel the urgency to speed up, that is typically the instant we need to slow down. Often when we feel the impulse to flee, it is the opportunity to face ourselves."

I don't know about you, but I can think of so many times in my life when I have reacted to fear and anxiety by doing all of these things—holding on, speeding up, removing myself. I know for a while I hung on to my marriage out of fear. I called it loyalty or commitment, but I see now that it was just my old, needy neighbor. I was afraid of being seen as a failure, afraid of emotionally damaging my children, afraid of not being able to support myself, and afraid of starting over.

Unfortunately, being steeped in feelings of fear within that relationship has created a pattern—a conditioned response of fear around all romantic relationships. The only man I have allowed myself to want since my divorce is someone who, quite conveniently, will never let me close. I hide here in plain sight—emotionally unavailable, on account of wanting someone who is emotionally unavailable. How clever of me. Because if I were to risk my heart with someone who is actually eager to take it, I might make the same mistakes. I am afraid I will think I know someone, then find out I don't. I'm afraid of rejection. I am afraid of that cold, painful purgatory where love is replaced by obligation, and bitterness is all we can taste on our tongues.

Fear knocks on my door whenever I so much as *think* about risking myself in this way. She considers herself to be an expert on the topic of love. She has twisted love and fear up in my head so insidiously that I almost believe they are the same.

But I know something she doesn't.

I know that when the right person arrives, I'll muster the courage to introduce him to her (it's only polite, after all). I suspect he'll make an introduction of his own—of his fear, to mine. Perhaps our fears will keep each other company, and they will be less likely to pop in on us out of the blue. And when they do show up, I hope we will try ... *"to let go when the urge is to hold tightly, to slow down when the urge is to speed up, and to stay when the impulse is to flee."*

I hope we will use our fear as an opportunity to face ourselves, together.

(You Don't Have
To) Do It Yourself

My mother's cancer diagnosis caught her (and the rest of us) completely by surprise. She had not felt the least bit ill. It was odd explaining to my daughters that their Nana was sick. She certainly didn't *look* sick.

As time went on, the chemo treatments did what the cancer had not. It's surreal, watching the nurses don smocks and gloves to protect themselves from the very concoction that will soon deliberately course through my mother's veins. "We aren't supposed to come into direct contact with it," the nurse explains, without even a touch of irony, as she hooks the bag of poison up to my mother's chest.

I've had to explain to my girls that it is the medicine that is making Nana feel sick, but that it is also going to make her better. I've reassured them that, when my mom stops getting the medicine, she will feel well again. It's a bizarre concept, one that I can't really expect my daughters to understand. Even I have been worried that it isn't *just* the chemo.

After Mom ended up in the hospital in need of a blood transfusion, the doctors decided to suspend the chemo protocol for an extra week. We were all scared by how sick she got, and we felt a mixture of relief and disappointment that her treatments would have to extend a week further into February.

We knew she needed a break, but we all just want it to be over— especially my mother. In the end, the week off ended up being a real gift. She actually had the opportunity to feel well. This is a woman who is accustomed to being in perpetual motion; who never ceases to amaze me with her passion for do-it-yourself home improvement projects of all sizes.

Lately she has felt winded simply by walking from one room to another. So, you can imagine what a wonderful surprise it was when one morning this week, I walked into her house to find that she had been repainting her living room—changing the wall color and adding an accent color on the fireplace mantle. "I have never liked this wall color," she announced, pleased with herself. "It's too green. And the fireplace is supposed to be a focal point, so I'm finally going to put in a gas insert."

In that moment I could have cried from relief and joy. To see that it was actually true, what I'd told my girls. It really *was* the chemo that was making her feel so sick, and she will feel better when it's over. (The tests show it's working, too).

Yesterday she started back up again with the chemo. Two more treatments spread over four weeks. We know what to expect this time. We know it will take all of her strength to get to the other side of this. It'll be an all-hands-on-deck kind of month. She will not have to do this particular "improvement" project herself—but I have no doubt she will get back to her serious DIY backlog when all of this is behind her. Cheers to that.

The Spaces In Between

Life is quite a roller coaster. I love the highs. And I have (albeit somewhat begrudgingly) come to appreciate the lows too, as they have been my greatest teachers.

It isn't all peaks and valleys, though—this thing called living. In fact, we do most of our living in the space *between* suffering and elation.

So, what of that? How do we feel in the space between? Do we even notice?

The other night, I was walking down the short hallway between the two bedrooms of my children. I had just tucked Beau in, and I was headed to do the same for Ruby. It's a walk I have taken—a task I have done—thousands of times.

On this particular, unremarkable evening, there in the darkened hallway, I felt a sudden wave of contentment wash over me. I stopped, and I thought to myself, *this is my life.*

It took my breath away—my gratitude in that completely ordinary, everyday moment.

Our lives are filled with highs and lows, but the real beauty of it is this—the "sweet spots" can be found, most days, in the most unlooked-for of places … in the spaces in between.

Can You Still
Hold Me?

"Pick me up," Ruby said, looking up at me and smiling.

It struck me that she hadn't asked me to do that in a long time—and that eyeing this suddenly, impossibly big girl before me, I didn't know if I could. Something about the way she looked at me told me that she wondered the same.

Mom, can you still hold me?

Time is funny that way. You don't notice it stealing from you until every so often, you do. I could, technically, pick her up—if, say, she was injured or in danger. I have no doubt that my Mama Bear strength would kick in. I'd be able to lift her straight over my head if I needed to protect her. Even in a non-emergency I guess I could, if I remembered to lift with my knees and to brace myself. But the truth is, my baby isn't a baby anymore.

I wondered: When was the last time I easily and mindlessly hoisted her onto my hip while I multitasked? The thief called Time is *so* stealth—she lulls us to sleep with our busyness while ever-so-gently easing our babies from our hips, untangling their fingers from our hair, and presenting us with new versions of our most treasured beings.

We love them just as much, but we can't help but search their faces for the babies they've replaced.

Mom, can you still hold me?

Be Here (and Here, and Here) Now

"You look as though you could use a minute to gather yourself," Beau's piano teacher said as I somewhat breathlessly presented my daughter, ten minutes late for her lesson and without the instruction book we were asked to bring.

Indeed, I could.

The two of them went off to the practice space while I plopped myself on her couch and exhaled. As I sat, I felt my frenetic energy pulsing and swirling around me.

Granted, the past couple of hours had been particularly chaotic. I had to scramble when, suddenly, plans changed and I found myself needing to be in two places at once. (I still haven't mastered that, but I will let you know when I figure it out).

Still, I couldn't blame my swirling mind entirely on that, for it had been running at a dizzying pace all day. I realized that within each moment I had been anticipating the next ... and the next. Some days are like that, I know. Actually, I seem to struggle with this a lot.

I love the phrase, *be here now.* I want to be present in my life, and yet on most days there are so many tasks strung together that I am living in a constant state of anticipation. It feels as though if I'm not perpetually poised for the next thing, everything could be derailed. Things may be overlooked, or forgotten ... or I may even find myself needing to be in two places at once!

Wait a minute.

Things *do* get overlooked and forgotten. And I *do* find myself needing to be in two places at once—even when I am living in this *what's next, what's next, what's next* state of mind. So maybe I am not actually helping myself by feeding my brain with the never-ending adrenaline rush of, "Don't mess up!"

In fact, maybe if I stopped worrying so much about—oh, I don't know, *all the things*—I might find myself being far more productive, and even (gasp!) happier.

The Rapids

I was twelve years old when I first understood that my mother would do anything for her children, without hesitation. In fact, she would drown.

The creek near our house, often completely dry, sometimes offered a gentle current into which we could dip our toes. But on this day, it was raging. I had never seen it that way before, nor have I ever since. I remember rounding the corner to the place where my younger brother, Ryan, and our friend, Sarah, were playing. Ryan, with the recklessly foolish courage of a seven-year-old boy, was attempting to cross the rushing water. He placed his foot on a partially submerged rock, slipped and went under.

It wasn't as if I saw him float away. There were no flailing arms reaching up. There was no possible hope of grabbing ahold of him. He was just ... gone.

I ran as fast as I could up the hill to our house. I burst into the bathroom where my mother was in the shower, and I screamed at her, "Ryan fell into the creek!"

"What?" she yelled, not comprehending my words.

"RYAN! THE CREEK!"

I remember running down the hill after her. She was partially naked, throwing clothes on as she ran.

"Where?" she screamed, looking frantically for any sign of him. The sound of the rushing water was deafening.

"There!" I yelled, pointing helplessly and uselessly to the spot where I last saw him. There was no sign of him, but if he was in there, she was going in too. I watched as she jumped into the rushing water. She immediately disappeared beneath the water's surface, just as he had. I stood there, frozen.

What we didn't know was that by the time my mother jumped into the water, Ryan had already come out. Downstream and out of sight, the creek widened and the current lessened. Ryan was able to stand up and walk right out. He was dazed and had a gash on his head, but otherwise he was fine. In shock, he had wandered out into the road where a neighbor had discovered him, soaking wet and bleeding.

When my mother emerged from the water downstream in the same place, Ryan was already gone. Devastated, she was certain he had drowned. You can imagine the hysterically tearful reunion moments later. I remember watching my mother, soaking wet, sobbing and clutching her youngest son as an EMT examined the cut on his head. Looking at the raging creek, no one could believe they had both survived. I understood then that Mom would willingly give her life for any one of us.

I have thought of this story often during my mother's battle with cancer. There really is no way to thank someone for loving you more than anyone else ever could. There is no way to properly express gratitude to someone who would jump into the rapids for you. Except maybe … if there comes a time when she is being pulled under, I can show her that I am willing to jump in after her, too.

To Love

The world lost a beautiful man last night—my friend, Jaime. I struggle writing this; it just seems so wrong, writing about him in the past tense. I want to write "he is" and I have to go back and correct myself: "he *was*." It seems impossible that someone who shone so brightly could leave us so soon.

I remember a story about when Jaime met Melissa, his future wife. He told her that his name was spelled Jaime (rather than Jamie), because "J'aime" means "I love" in French. Honestly, we had a good laugh about that, because—come on! What a line! But the thing about Jaime was—although I'm sure he delivered this explanation of his name with a grin and a twinkle in his eye—it was the truth. *He loved.*

The love and devotion that Melissa and Jaime had for each other was a joy to witness. They still looked at each other like people in love. They had fun. They made each other laugh every day—even on the terrible ones.

Jaime was so proud of each of his children. He always smiled broadly whenever he spoke of them. *He loved.*

If you were talking to Jaime, you had his full attention. Nothing was more important to him in that moment than giving you his time. He listened. He had a way of making everyone who knew him feel like they were important to him—because they were. We all were. *He loved.*

Over the years I have heard so many stories about things that Jaime did or said to help others. None of these stories did I ever hear from Jaime. Not one. He was so humble. Nothing he did was ever for recognition or even for a thank you. He did those things because that was who he was. He knew no other way to be. *He loved.*

I see so many parallels between Jaime and my father—their clever humor, their humility, their kindness, their devotion, their generosity, their quiet good deeds.

They loved.

Lightbulb Triage

I have needed to buy light bulbs for a few months now. I am certain I have been in stores that sell light bulbs many times during this period. I am also certain that I can afford to purchase light bulbs. Therefore, access to light bulbs is not an issue for me. And yet, I do not ever remember that I need light bulbs while I am in the general vicinity of light bulbs. As a result, I have a bit of a lighting triage situation in my home.

I keep "borrowing" light from one lamp in the house to illuminate another. No, I don't carry one bulb from room to room—it hasn't gotten that bad (yet). The girls and I use torches, obviously.

Really what happens is this: A light bulb goes out, and I consider which lamp in the house is the least important. I then remove the bulb from that lamp to use in the other. At the moment I have two lamps that have been deemed "non-critical"—forcing them to sacrifice their light to areas with more urgent or frequent need.

It occurs to me that perhaps the lighting situation in my house is not unlike the illumination of my brain. Perhaps it is just not possible for me to have all of the areas of my brain lit all at once. Perhaps it's okay to choose which areas are most in need of my energy at any given moment and to let other areas remain, at least temporarily, at rest.

Besides, if too many areas are lit up at once, it's bound to be a real drain on my natural resources. Clearly, I need as many resources as possible—so I can remember to buy light bulbs.

Spoons

Today Jaime was laid to rest. It was incredibly touching to see the community of support around his family, and to bear witness as we all tried our best to collectively shoulder the enormous weight of our grief. Honestly, I was completely wrecked by his grieving children, who must live with the cruel paradox of having had the most wonderful father for not nearly long enough. Jaime was young and vibrant and had so much love to give.

After the service (burial, collation ...), I felt exhausted in the way that only emotions can exhaust a person. When I got home, I told my girls, who had been home with a sitter, that I needed to lie down for a few minutes. I went into my room and laid on my bed, curling up on my side and closing my eyes.

Moments later, Ruby came into the room. She climbed onto the bed, and laid down with her back to me, shimmying herself into the hollow I'd formed with my curled-up body. Next, Beau climbed in behind me, pressing herself into my back, and reaching for my hand. No one spoke.

Then, for the first time in years, the three of us took a nap.

Failure Is an Option

"So ... *you failed?*" asked Beau.

I had signed up for "40 Days to Personal Revolution," a program through my yoga studio based on a book by Baron Baptiste.

First of all, I probably had no business signing up for it to begin with. The commitment is forty consecutive days of yoga and meditation. For someone who has been as sadly lethargic as I have been recently, forty consecutive days of heated power yoga is a lofty goal. Not to mention the time commitment. Nevertheless, I decided to give it a go.

When I walked in the door from Jaime's service, Beau asked me when I was going to go to yoga. (The kids have been really into watching me mark each successful day on the calendar. They are excellent cheerleaders.)

"I'm not," I said, exhausted.

"So ... *you failed?*"

I felt a quick flash of defensiveness—a need to justify my failure. Then I realized, it is good for them to see me "fail," because for God's sake, it happens a hell of a lot. Why shrink away from that reality?

More to the point, why get defensive? What I should feel is proud, or at the very least, unfazed, because failure is *not the same* as quitting. I'd like my kids to learn this as soon as possible. We can fail a million times in a million different ways, and it is not the same as giving up. In fact, having failed a lot means we kept trying.

So, I looked her in the eye and said, "Yup, I failed. But guess what? I get to try again tomorrow—and the day after that, and the day after that."

Show Up

At the moment, my words are completely inadequate. My forty-four-year-old friend is a widow. A widow and a single mother of four. Life is so cruel sometimes.

I have written about how we do ourselves and others a disservice by comparing our pain (or our cause of pain) with that of others. I have said that grief is grief, and loss is loss. We feel how we feel. They feel how they feel. Everyone's feelings are valid and true, regardless of whether we perceive someone as having more or less reason to suffer than we do. As with anything in life, comparing ourselves to others in any way does not serve us.

While I still believe that to be true, sometimes I just can't help it. As I watched Melissa and Jaime's children's faces as their father was lowered into the earth, I felt emotionally gutted. I couldn't help but think, I had *three decades* longer with my wonderful father than these children had with theirs. My pain is enormous. What of theirs? Can I even imagine?

As for my friend, she lost the person with whom she planned to happily spend the rest of her life. The life she is living, they built it together over the course of more than twenty years. Everything in her home whispers a story about Jaime. He is everywhere and nowhere all at once.

I feel intimidated by the grief I imagine she holds within her. I am not proud of that, but I will own it, because I know my discomfort comes from a desire to relieve her pain, coupled with a deep knowing that I can't possibly do that for her. Her pain is hers to process, and she is so incredibly strong and capable.

That being said, I can show up for her anyway. I can show up even when I know I can't take away the pain. I can show up to witness her in her grief. I can show up for the hard and messy and complicated stuff that lands heavily and mercilessly after the dust settles.

Are You Really Okay?

Once, when I was twenty-two, I was duct taped to a board for several hours.

Okay fine, I am sure it wasn't actually duct tape. It could have been some kind of a strap, I suppose—and *maybe* it was actually some kind of spinal board EMTs use. It probably wasn't a couple of hours, either, but it sure felt that way.

I had been in a car accident—a really bad car accident. I was hit nearly head on at a four-way intersection, causing my car to do a 180. The whole front end of my car was crumpled like a tin can. Later, when my Uncle Ed saw the car, all he could say was "Holy. *Shit*."

I was alone in the car. People came running, yelling, "Are you okay? Don't move!"

I remember thinking, "I don't know. *Am* I okay?" It didn't seem to anyone present (including, for a moment—me) that I possibly could be. I did a full body scan—ten fingers, ten toes, limbs still attached and intact, no apparent hemorrhaging ...

"Uh ... yes? Yes. Yes! I am okay! I am!"

(They didn't believe me.)

When the paramedics arrived, despite my claims that I was fine, they duct taped me to a board. (That's my story, and I'm sticking to it). One line of tape went across my forehead so I couldn't turn my head, another across my upper arms, and then one across my hips.

At the hospital, I was placed in a holding room. I was still attached to the board, which was now on top of a gurney. It seemed like forever that I was in there, all alone, unable to move. That part felt scary.

A nurse came in and asked me who they should call. I was near-est my Aunt Anne and Uncle Ed's house in a different state, so I said they should call them instead of my parents. I knew my aunt would lose it if she got a cold call from the hospital about my having been in an accident, so I insisted that the nurse dial the number and hold the phone up to my face so I could tell her for myself.

"Hi, Aunt Anne. I am okay, but I had an accident and I'm at the hospital." On the other end of the line, I heard a gasp and then, "Oh Dear." (Classic Anne.)

I could feel the tears streaming down my face and collecting in my ears, because I could not turn my head nor lift my arms to wipe the tears away.

"Really, I'm okay," I reiterated. "I'm just … duct taped to a board."

I was sore for a few days, but no worse for the wear, as they say. Unfortunately, the same could not be said for my car.

I couldn't help but think of this story today. This morning I woke up with two little girls in my bed; as usual, they had snuck in with me in the night and snuggled up to me on either side. I lay there for a while, just thinking about the amazing little beings they are. My God, I love them so much. I thought about everything they have had thrown at them in the past few years. Frankly, it seems like enough to have done some pretty serious damage. There was their parents' divorce, the death of their Papa, their Nana battling cancer—and then there's the matter of their dad revealing she is really a woman. These are not small things. I wonder, are my girls really okay? Really?

Like my accident, it seems nearly impossible for them to walk away from (or through) all of this unscathed. *Shouldn't I be duct taping them to a board or something?!*

I am still pondering this at the bus stop, where I find myself bringing the question to my friend, Michelle. "Are my kids really okay? They seem okay. Is that really the truth?"

Never one to shrink from a question, she kindly reminds me of a few important things.

First, my girls are more than okay. They are incredible.

Second, life's challenges build compassion, gratitude, and perspective.

Third, knowing that someone has their back, come hell or high water, is what makes all the difference. It isn't about what a child goes through, as much as it is about them knowing they never have to do it alone.

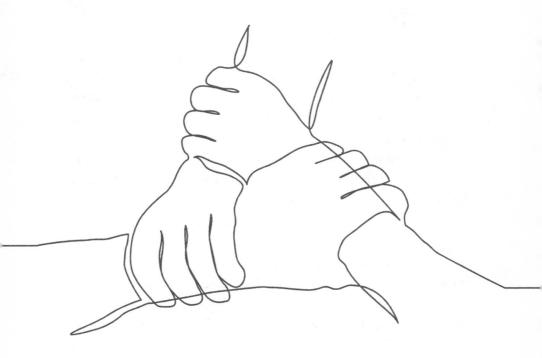

A Nice Ring to It

The other day, while at breakfast with friends, I noticed that one of them was wearing a really beautiful engagement ring. She has been married for a couple of years now, so the ring wasn't the news of the day or anything—I just happened to notice it at that moment. It made me think of my own beautiful engagement ring, tucked away for over four years now (on account of the whole not-being-married-anymore thing).

I really love my ring—or at least, I did. I did when I said, "I do." It was bright and beautiful, just like I hoped my marriage would be.

Funny, I don't remember taking it off for the last time to stow it away. This seems a little sad in hindsight. Like it should have been as impactful a moment as the one in which I first slid it on.

I decided that when I got home, I was going to dig it out and wear it again. I could wear it on my right hand. Why not? It seemed like a waste to keep such a beautiful piece of jewelry hidden away. After all, it is just a thing—a material object.

Except when it isn't.

My mother has been wearing my father's wedding band since he passed away over a year ago. Melissa wears Jaime's ring as well, on a chain around her neck. These "things" symbolize something beautiful when they represent a marriage that has endured.

So, what of a marriage that hasn't?

I'll admit, I had already drafted in my head what I was going to write before I even dug out the ring. I would write about how I am so evolved and healed now that when I look at this beautiful ring,

I am only reminded of the beautiful parts of my marriage. (Insert eye roll.) Ah yes, I would celebrate the love with which the ring was given and received by wearing it proudly.

Then I put it on … and that lasted about an hour, tops.

As much as I can reflect on my marriage and fully appreciate the beautiful bits (especially the two beautiful bits tucked into their beds as I write this)—for me, my ring now symbolizes hurt, disappointment, failure, confusion, and sadness.

These are not feelings I wish to conjure every time I look down at my ring, regardless of whether it is the left hand or the right. I have done a lot of inner work and healing over the past few years. When I look at the person I married, she does not evoke in me the same negative feelings conjured by the ring. We've moved on. We parent well together. We still laugh quite a bit. There is love.

But that ring. *Ugh.*

I just can't imagine a day when that ring is going to conjure happy thoughts for me. It's sad but true: that once bright and beautiful, and now tarnished, ring can never again be just a thing.

Not to me.

Metaphorical Ball

I was doing some work on my computer while my dog, Louie, was experiencing yet another existential crisis: he desperately wanted to play catch with me, but was not willing to let me have the ball.

This exchange got me thinking about control, and how grabbing ahold of (or pushing away) something so fiercely can sometimes rob us of the joy of having it in our life. I thought about romantic love. Perhaps the ball is a metaphor for all of the love that I have—I mean, that *Louie* has—to give. Innately, he wants to share it with someone else. Yet he won't risk it. *What if they don't give it back?*

I have this comfort zone of people whom I love and trust—it is a truly rich and wonderful place. The idea of widening it feels … unnerving. It seems like whenever I get a little optimistic about my readiness to do so, I get tested, and I retreat, hastily.

I met a man a few weeks ago. We hit it off and exchanged phone numbers, but by the time I got home I had already talked myself out of wanting to see him again. He hadn't asked me to love him, nor to let him love me. He hadn't even asked me to go for a cup of coffee yet—but in my head I was already saying no to all of the above.

I was confused by my strong negative reaction after such a fun first encounter. I honestly wasn't sure whether I was being intuitive—that I just *knew* on some level that this guy was not for me—or just being a huge chicken. I suspected the latter. Nevertheless, he failed to meet the expectations of how I thought he should behave (via text, no less). End of story. Perhaps I dodged a bullet, or perhaps it was a bit of a self-fulfilled prophecy. I'll never know, because I didn't even give him a chance. Not really.

I am not sad about this. I'm actually relieved—which, considering I do wish to have a relationship again in this lifetime, is a bit concerning. Although I'd like to think that, when the right person comes along, it will be somewhat impossible for me to fumble.

While I was turning this over in my mind, I remembered this quote from Rachel Naomi Remen, M.D. *"Sooner or later we will come to the edge of all that we can control and find life, waiting there for us."*

There is a beautiful, rich life waiting for us—for Louie and me—as soon as we release control. Maybe—when we are willing and able to let go of the metaphorical ball.

Yogi Wisdom

I have practiced heated power yoga twenty-three out of the last twenty-five days, and I feel strong for the first time in forever. When I wake up in the morning, I can actually feel myself solidly present in my body before my mind starts to greet the day with a list of who, what, where and when. It has been so good for me.

Today I practiced in a room full of people. I was in the far back corner and we were holding a pose that required us to twist our bodies in the direction of the corner of the room in which I was positioned. While we were in this pose, I could not see anyone else, even in my periphery—only the wall. It was the type of pose in which after holding it for a while, my leg muscles burn, and I start saying some really nasty things to my teacher in my head. (It's okay, she knows—and she loves me anyway).

There I was, holding this pose for what seemed like an eternity. I was cursing up a storm in my head, so mad at her for *doing this to me*. So caught up was I in this story that I failed to notice she had called not one, but *two* other poses while I was holding that one twist.

Eventually I realized that everyone else had moved on, while I—in my blind corner, wallowing in my story of teacher brutality—did not even notice that I was suffering in a hell entirely of my own making.

I had to laugh. How often do we do this to ourselves in life? We get stuck somewhere—in a place, or an idea—and so focused are we on our suffering that we fail to notice that we do not need to be there anymore. We are the ones holding ourselves prisoner. We lose sight of the fact that we are free to move on.

Wide-Eyed Wonder

Yesterday's snow was thick and heavy, as it often is in March. It clung to everything, making for a beautiful, luminous sight this morning. After I brought the girls to the bus stop, I felt called to the woods. There is something about being the first person to walk on a snow-covered trail, with only deer tracks ahead of you, that is pure magic.

Walking in nature has almost always been a family endeavor for me. I have such fond memories of walks through the woods with my dad especially, and with extended family, and of course, with my girls.

I have grown to love my solitary walks as well. The woods are my church, and there have been many times when, within them, I have found myself inspired, uplifted, and soothed. Maybe I've just found myself, period. Today, however, as I walked within this winter wonderland, I found myself wishing there was someone there to see it with me. It was so perfect—so quiet. Everywhere I looked, the world glimmered.

I thought about that philosophical question: *"If a tree falls in the woods and no one is there to hear it, does it still make a sound?"*

I wondered—*if the woods are magical, and no one is here to witness it with me, did I still see it?*

I became aware that I had been walking this entire time with a huge smile on my face. In that moment, I knew it didn't matter whether anyone else was there. This walk was magical. I was grateful to bear witness.

This evening, as I sat down to write, I could hear two owls right outside my house, calling to each other.

Who-who—who-who-whooooooo! Who-who—who-who-whooooooo!

They sounded so close. I went to the bottom of the stairs and called to the four little girls playing board games upstairs. My daughters are having their first double sleepover.

"Girls, come here!"

The four of them appeared at the top of the stairs, no doubt thinking, *lights out already?*

"Come here, very quietly, and listen," I said. We crept to the front door and huddled together as I held the door open to the crisp night air. They looked at me expectantly.

"Just wait," I whispered.

Who-who—who-who-whooooooo! Who-who—who-who-whooooooo!

The girls exchanged wide-eyed glances, and grinned enormous, silent grins. I don't need someone else here to make the world's magic real—just noticing it makes it so. But sometimes, there's nothing better than having someone (or four wide-eyed, grinning someones) there to experience the magic with me.

Your Father's Favorite

It hit me today, unexpectedly and with the sudden force of a freight train.

I was sitting in my parents' house having coffee with my mother. Having spent the night, I was enjoying a cozy and relaxed morning in my pajamas. She pointed to a large photograph behind me on the wall and said, "I should probably change that to something more recent. Will was only five in that picture, so it is more than a decade old. But it was your father's favorite."

Your father's favorite.

That's all it took to knock the wind out of me. This surprised me. While I think about my father every single day, it doesn't rattle me as often—not like this. If anything, I have found a new way to be with him. I have been talking to him a lot. Of course, he probably thinks I only call on him when I need something—typical kid. (Okay, maybe praying for him to help me make it to the gas station on fumes was an abuse of his potential on the other side—although I did make it. Thanks, Dad.)

Back to this morning … *your father's favorite.* There I was, about to dissolve into a puddle. For a panicked second, I considered making a dash for the bathroom before the floodgates opened. I thought, *I should protect my mother from my pain. She doesn't need this, not right now with all of her worries*—but it was too late.

"What did I say?" she asked, "Is it … Dad?"

I nodded my head yes. "Sometimes I just expect him to come walking around the corner," I said, tears streaming down. "I wish he were here right now."

"I know what you mean," she said, gently. "I still think it's him whenever the phone rings or whenever someone pulls into the driveway."

I couldn't help but imagine the small death she must feel every single time she remembers that isn't possible.

As if reading my thoughts, she said, "He's still very much here."

My mind flashed back to a conversation we'd had a few months after he died. Trying to comfort her, I had said that very thing: "He is still here."

Somewhat angrily (and justifiably so) she'd replied, "What good is it for him to be 'here' if he can't be *here*?"

I felt a slight sense of relief now—glad that she has since found some peace within his transition into Spirit. I wondered what it is like to live with a ghost.

Then I realized, I already know.

Plant Your Own Garden

"Mom, do we have any wrapping paper?" Ruby asks.

"Sure. Who is the present for?"

"Oh, it's for me!" she says, eyes wide and twinkling. "I am going to put it *way* under my bed. And then I am going to try to forget all about it. Then one day, when I'm cleaning my room, I'll be *so excited* to find it!"

Google Is an Asshole

"I am concerned about two areas on the lung x-ray that look as though they could be related to the cancer," he said.

What I heard was, "Your mother now has lung cancer."

Wait! She just finished chemo. How can she have new cancer already?

I used to be an eternal optimist. Even now, I can pull out an "Everything is going to be fine!" but lately ... maybe it's my recent life experiences, or just getting older, but I have begun to brace myself for the worst. As I sat there across from this unknown doctor, my mother lying between us on the bed in the emergency room, I was sure I was hearing what he *wasn't* saying. What he was trying to tell me with his eyes, which was: *This. Is. Bad.*

We weren't even supposed to be there. More than two weeks out from her very last chemo—*we were on a break!* A month off before phase two, the big surgery.

But her body had different plans. She spiked a fever and protocol had her going straight to the ER. They ran all kinds of tests to make sure she didn't have an infection, the flu, pneumonia. She had none of these things. In fact, they saw no reason to keep her there, so it was, *"Go home, get some rest, drink lots of fluids—oh, and you might be dying. Better get that checked out as soon as possible. Have a nice day!"*

I thought about those stories you hear—about the people who find out they have a brain tumor only because they hit their head and needed an x-ray. You have to believe that it was divine intervention. At least, I do. A higher power wanted it to be known. Applying that logic, I thought, *Mom surely has lung cancer.* That's why she ended up coming to the ER and getting a chest x-ray for seemingly no reason. A higher power wanted us to know what was there.

And so, it began. Waiting to get in for a test. Waiting for results. *She might be dying. Have a nice day.*

Waiting to get in for a different test. Waiting for these results. *She might be dying. Have a nice day.*

This continued for an entire month. And so, the month of reprieve between chemo and surgery turned out to be anything but. While she did feel better physically, the testing and the waiting—oh, the waiting—was brutal. Trying to act normal when our minds kept creeping over to the darkest places. Trying to stay with what was known and to not go crazy thinking about what was not. My mother and I joked that, if we got bad news, we might look back on these awful days of waiting as "the good ole' days." She quoted Bob Dylan: *"I wish I didn't know now what I didn't know then."*

The doctors told us that if my mother's cancer had metastasized to the lungs, she would not be having the trifecta of surgical "ectomies" that were planned. We did not ask what the new plan would be. I had read, before we'd even left the ER that day, that breast cancer metastasized to the lung is, in fact, terminal.

Sometimes Google is such an asshole.

And so, we waited.

Jedi Mind Trick

It's a funny thing that happens—a Jedi Mind Trick of sorts. While we waited for Mom's test results, we found ourselves *hoping* that she was going to be having major surgery. Something as scary as a five-hour surgery suddenly seemed like a trip to Disney when compared to the alternative with which we were presented. And so, things went down something like this:

You might have terminal lung cancer; in which case you won't be having surgery.

Just kidding, you don't have lung cancer! You get to have surgery!

Yay! That's amazing! Thank you!

Mom's lungs were clear, and for a couple of days we basked in the glow of finally having gotten some good news. Even though we had been put through the ringer to get it.

For me, the euphoria lasted until yesterday—one day pre-op. I started to feel restless and jittery. I slept fitfully last night. This morning, Mom and I awoke in the dark and had a mostly silent pre-dawn ride to the hospital. The intake room was chaos as they readied all of the 8:00 a.m. surgical patients at once. Mom winced as a nurse grazed her IVs trying to get the blood pressure cuff on. I felt a surge of protectiveness. No matter how strong you know a person to be, when they are lying on an ambulatory bed wearing a surgical cap and johnny, they look helpless ... and scared—rightfully so.

The nurse was frustrated because the number on my mother's ID didn't match her file. There was a computer glitch. "Sorry for the delay," she said. "We want to get that fixed before she goes into surgery."

"Uh … yeah," I replied, "I don't want to come back and find out you've amputated her leg."

Mom and I cracked up. We needed that, but the nurse was not amused. Perhaps dark humor is not her thing. Maybe it's an acquired taste, although it seems like the professionals in certain fields need to appreciate it to survive.

Come to think of it, the funeral director didn't appreciate my dark humor either. A year ago, when we asked if our family dog could be buried with my dad, the director had said, "The dog has been cremated, I assume." To which I replied, "Oh, the dog isn't dead. It's just that Dad was the only one who liked her."

Sometimes laughter is the only thing that keeps me sane, and I know a person is a part of my tribe when they go to dark places with it.

As I sit here writing this, Mom is in the recovery room. They are letting the anesthesia wear off before I can see her. Everything went well, they said. I am so relieved.

Her leg should heal up just fine.

Stay in Your Own
Hula Hoop

Is there anything more confounding at times than human relationships? Ironically—or perhaps, cruelly?—I believe that navigating these emotional labyrinths is the sole reason for our existence. It is a life-long endeavor to understand one another, and doing so requires us to learn how to communicate. How to speak, and how to listen. How to ask the right questions, rather than making assumptions.

Making assumptions is so much easier, though! We don't need any help from anyone else—we can do this all by ourselves! And assumptions are so helpful—like, when we want to needlessly get ourselves spun up. I hate to brag, but I'm kind of a master at assuming what people's motivations are for their actions and reactions.

I said that stupid thing and now he thinks ...
I forgot to do that thing, and now she thinks ...
He obviously hates me and that's why he ...
He must have done that because ...
She must have responded that way because ...

This is when Monica will remind me to "stay in my own hula hoop." Meaning, I only know what I know, and I only feel what I feel. Still, isn't it awesome when we presume to know what other people's innermost thoughts and motivations are without—oh I don't know—*asking* them?

You'd think I'd be skilled at this, being as I pour my heart out in my writing every day, but the reality is, *this* is my hula hoop, right here. Writing about my feelings is a one-sided endeavor—a completely controlled experience by the soft glow of my computer.

So, I hereby challenge myself to stretch my muscles of understanding—to open my mouth and ask, *"How do you feel? Why do you feel that way? Can you tell me the reason you did that? I want to understand."* It is sort of the holy grail of loving relationships, after all—to be understood, to understand, and to not make shit up in your head about what people think and why they do what they do. Just ask.

I deeply appreciate the people in my life who are willing to engage with me in this way. When a person can connect with themselves and give a thoughtful response to the question, "Why?" it takes my breath away. I feel humbled and grateful to know someone else's truth. It is so brave to say, *"Yes, I want you to know me, to truly know my heart. I trust you to try to understand me, even if you may not like what I have to say."* In a way, it feels like magic—*you mean, all I have to do is ask and you'll tell me what lies within you?* It can't possibly be that easy. Yet, with some people, it is.

With others, we are still left to draw our own conclusions. Not everyone is ready or willing or able to delve into why they said what they said, or why they did what they did, let alone what those things might mean. We can ask, but that doesn't mean we will get an answer with any real depth to it. When this happens, perspective and compassion are useful tools—but in using them, we must always remember that we are drawing our own conclusion, based only on our own perceptions, from within our own hula hoop. Our conclusions can help us navigate the moment, but that doesn't make them true.

Also, some questions simply need breathing space. They require our patience. The answers are not always immediately clear. There are some questions we are not ready to answer, and some answers we are not ready to hear.

Spring Will
Come Again

We are nearly a month into what the calendar calls "spring," and it is cold outside—really fucking cold. And, just to add insult to injury, it is also windy as hell. (Is hell windy? Probably not, I just really feel like cursing today, damn it.)

Actually, I am in a perfectly fine mood, albeit begrudging of Winter for overstaying his welcome. The howling wind outside makes me want to continue to turn inward, when what I want to be feeling this time of year is an opening—a blossoming, a gesture of expansion. I want to be bursting with warmth and joy, damn it.

I know, I know, warmth and joy should be found within, regardless of whether the weather is cooperating. But seriously, my vision of spring does *not* include wool socks. And yet, yesterday … ah, yesterday was beautiful, and perhaps twenty degrees warmer. The sun shone. I was at long last liberated from my winter coat. Fleeting as that taste of spring was, it was a reminder that winter won't last forever. (It never does, you know.)

Such is life. Sometimes the cold hangs around longer than we would wish. Sometimes it appears to leave, only to come rushing back. A frigid gust shocks us just when we have dared to shed our protective layers. But always, it relents. It must, for the cold is not sustainable and—in knowing this, we must also understand, neither is the warmth. We cycle through them, again and again. We endure, and expand, and endure again.

So, I will curl inward for another day, and wait. Spring will come again.

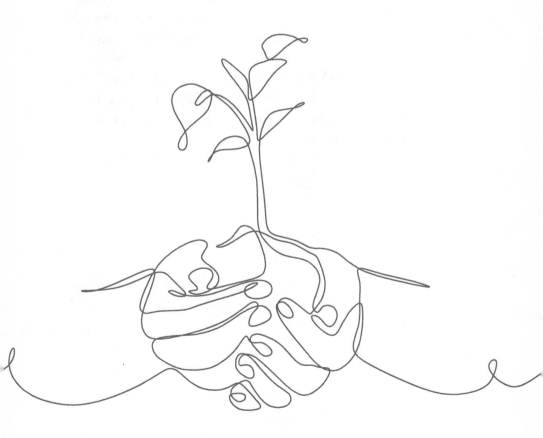

Her Lens

My mother's photography is how she expresses her love of the world—of her world—to all of us. It is her.

After Dad died, and she was diagnosed with cancer, she fought. She struggled. And she did not pick up her camera for eight months. She did not share her view of the world. I think it was just too dark a place.

Late last month—April—she was given a clean bill of health. She is considered cancer-free. Florida-bound for our annual family trip, she brought her camera. Once again, she was ready to show us the world through her lens.

Grief, Interrupted

Our family trip to Florida last year—the first one without my father—was hard. I shied away from family photos. It was as if I didn't want to remember it.

No, not "as if," actually. I didn't want to remember. I just wanted to get through it, if only because he would want us to keep going.

For months prior to this year's trip, there was an unspoken worry. "*Will Mom be well enough to go? Will we go without her? Can we? (She will insist. It will be awful.)*"

As the trip approached, we learned that, not only would she be able to come, but she would also be completely done with treatments. We were elated. I was on a high for about a week—until suddenly the pain of not having my dad there resurfaced. In talking to my mom, the same thing had happened to her—elation, then grief.

Perhaps, she said, we never had enough time to grieve him. Suddenly we were thrown into dealing with The Big C. Our grieving was interrupted. Now that that storm has passed, the grief returns, not yet through with us. I found this incredibly frustrating. I know I'll mourn my dad forever, but I so desperately want to feel light again. Life has been so heavy. I want to stand on the beach with my toes in the warm sand and feel the sun on my face, both literally and metaphorically.

In the end, aside from a few tearful moments, the predominant feelings I have about this year's trip are those of gratitude and joy. Dad isn't here—but Mom is, and she had fought like hell to be here.

And here we were—my big, beautiful family, in the most beautiful place.

There's something I've noticed about the beach at Boca Grande. Every year, it is the same familiar place, but there is always something slightly different about it, too. All of the storms throughout the year, and even the day-to-day currents and tides, they alter the landscape. They erode and reshape the coastline. They create sand bars. Things never stay the same, and yet, it is always beautiful. It is always Boca.

In our lives, we have day-to-day currents and tides that ever so slowly and subtly alter us. Sometimes, there are big storms that ravage us, and we must rebuild. Sometimes, the devastation is so vast we aren't sure where to begin—but we do. We always do.

A Warm Pocket

It has been happening bit by bit, this change. Beau has stepped one tentative foot into her adolescence as the other foot is still carefully positioned in the land of childhood. Her dirty converse high tops straddle them both, not entirely belonging in either; existing in the in-between.

The metaphor I so readily conjure is that of a butterfly. The green and gold chrysalis that has housed her—protected her—has now become translucent, allowing a first look inside at the transformed being that is to come. This beautiful creature must soon emerge, becoming more and more constrained within the space that has kept her safe and warm. She is nearly ready to stretch her wings.

Part of me dreads this impending disconnection between us; my inevitable decline in importance in her world. At the same time, I await with great anticipation the young woman she will become. *Who is this butterfly meant to be? Will she stop and rest for a moment before taking flight? Will she stay close?*

When we learned of her upcoming school field trip, she told me it would be nice if I would come, but it would also be fine if I didn't. (One foot in, one foot out).

We don't have to leave for a couple of hours to where we'll meet her class, so we venture to the beach to let Louie romp. I smile as I watch Beau run with the same look of wild abandon as our dog, freed from the constraints of his leash. She flies—head back, hair wild, entirely unaffected by the presence of other beach goers.

Thinking of my own insanely insecure adolescent years, I wonder if she'll stay this way. I hope so.

Once worn out, she sidles up beside me. It is a beautiful, but crisp, late spring morning. I have my hands tucked into my jacket pockets for warmth, and as we walk, she slips her hand—still so small—into my pocket, intertwining her fingers with mine. We walk this way for a while, the two of us sharing a warm pocket.

Soon, it is time for the field trip. It is the first one I have been on in a couple of years, and I marveled at them all—this group of children. All so different, yet so connected. They are at that age where most of the girls tower over the boys. They move like a giggly, beautifully awkward amoeba. As we meander along, I keep my distance like a good mom-who-was-allowed-to-come-but-it's-okay-if-she-didn't. I watch as my daughter flits along with her friends, free and happy.

At one point I am surprised to find her walking along beside me and (I presume just by habit) she slides her hand into mine. Squeezing it, I look down at her and smile. Suddenly self-conscious, she offers a quick grin and lets go, running ahead to join her friends. As she should.

I will always have a warm pocket when she needs one.

Counting Heads

Lately I have been feeling really happy. Sunshine-y, even. I have been in a "Make sure you tell people you love them (not because you're afraid they're gonna die, but just because you love them)" kind of mood. A "random acts of kindness" kind of mood. A mood of expansion, a gesture of openness—a heart opened wide to life, and to love, and to the infinite possibilities of both.

I think it all started when we were in Florida. I experienced a shift. We were nearing the end of the trip—that time when everyone begins to dread leaving paradise to come home—and I had this revelation. "Home" for me is a pretty amazing place. In the most literal sense, we live in a beautiful town in coastal New England, and I have settled into a home that feels like a sanctuary to me. But home is more than a town, and more than a house. Home is my beautiful family. Home is my passionate work community. Home is my incredible friendships. Home is also within me. I am feeling more and more comfortable in my own skin. Home is truly a gift. I am beyond blessed; I see that. I feel that.

Going back to "reality" isn't so bad. In fact, reality is, at the moment, pretty damn good.

Throughout all of the challenges I have had, somewhere inside of me (sometimes way, way inside of me) I always knew that the darkness wouldn't last forever. Life is a pendulum after all, and things are always bound to swing the other way sooner or later.

Which is what worries me now, in my sunshine-y place. ("Ha! Will she ever relax?" you wonder? Umm, nope.) Now that my pendulum has swung toward happiness, I can't help this niggling feeling (or knowing) that the upswing can't last forever, either. It goes both ways, for better and for worse. That's how it works.

On the field trip with Beau's class, we went to the zoo. Throughout the trip I somewhat compulsively counted heads like a good chaperone, making sure everyone was safe and accounted for at any given moment—*One, two, three, four … Wait! We're missing one!*

Oh, nope—there she is. All good!

That's the best way I can think to describe this niggling. I feel like there's a little piece of my brain that is always actively "counting heads." Everyone I love can't possibly be safe and accounted for—so I count—*one, two, three, four. Really? All good? Can it be? Better count again, just to make sure …*

I don't know if I will ever stop counting heads. Major upheaval and loss will do that to a person. I'm okay with that. What I *am* learning to do is to enjoy the sunshine just the same. Right now, right here. I am home, and everyone is accounted for.

All good.

All the Colors

This weekend, we celebrated my mom's birthday. I've never been happier to celebrate someone's birthday. While still mourning my father, the fear that my mother might not survive breast cancer this year was real and visceral for all of us. Coming around to her birthday, cancer-free—was truly something to celebrate.

I got to thinking this morning about something I read once: *"What would you do differently if you knew you were dying?"* Well, guess what? You are!

I don't mean to be grim (smirk). The truth is, we are all inching toward death, every day. Of course, some of us have a lot longer to go than others—and this doesn't have as much to do with age as we'd like to think. Sure, we can take precautions. We can be smart. We can eat healthy, exercise, manage our stress, try our best not to run with scissors ... but beyond that, we don't have much control over our ultimate fate.

So, live every moment as if it's your last! Oh, you already know I am not going to say that. I have had enough hard knocks over the past couple of years to understand how unrealistic that is. I am not going to shame myself for my emotions. Sometimes we get hit hard and we reel from it. If I have a day when I just want to crawl back under the covers and hide (and, less likely, a day when it is even remotely possible to do that), I am going to go for it. I am not going to force myself to savor the day because it may be my last.

True contentment and joy are not forced. They are arrived at with grace. Grace for ourselves. Grace for everyone else—even, or especially, for the people who challenge us. Grace is not always an easy place to land. Sometimes it means processing our reactions. It means not stuffing them down under the guise of perpetually *enjoying the moment.* Sometimes we need time, space, and perspective.

If we can't possibly enjoy every moment, yet we are aware that the number of moments we are granted is never truly known, where does that leave us? I believe it leaves us in a place where we can appreciate the full experience of our humanity. We can allow ourselves to experience *all* of what it means to be human, as we strive to get to that place where there is no shame in feeling angry, sad, jealous, or afraid. And then, learning to release it all—because we can't stay there.

An image comes to me of an abstract painting. Can you imagine a piece of art that could convey all of the emotion of your life—no identifiable images, just colors. How would it look? Would you want the painting of your life to be monochromatic? Not me. I'd want it *all* to be there, messy and spilling out over the entire canvas—the light, the dark, the passion, the fear, the joy, everything.

Imagine looking closely at the painting of your life. Looking analytically. You could see the detail of each emotion, both the subtle and the dramatic shifts in hue. The colors would weave toward and away from each other, often overlapping, one spilling into the next. Then, if you were to stand back from it—when you take in the piece as a whole—you would truly see it. The whole of you; your whole life. You would see that all of the messy layers aren't random. In fact, they come together perfectly to evoke one very palpable and permeating emotion—Love.

The Fire You Build

We moved into our new house in October. It is the first house I've ever owned on my own. I love it so much. I feel so connected to it. Not to sound too woo-woo, but in a way, it feels like a physical manifestation of all of the work I've done—on myself, my family, my career—over the past few years. I truly feel that I created this place.

One of the best things about the house is that it has both a gas fireplace and a wood fireplace. The gas fireplace is just off the kitchen. There's a little love seat in front of it. It is a wonderful spot to sit with a cup of coffee on weekday mornings—in that dark, quiet hour between when I wake up and when the girls get up and we begin our chaotic sprint to work and school. I come downstairs and simply push a button—*click, whoosh*, instant coziness. When we leave for the day—*click, whoosh*, it's off.

This morning, I came downstairs and poured my coffee, but instead of *click, whoosh*, I went to the living room and started a real fire. I felt the texture of the firewood and remembered the paper knots my father taught me to make as kindling. The smell of the burning wood brings back fond memories of childhood.

As I sit here, enjoying my coffee, I can't help but notice how much more satisfying it is to sit by a fire that required more effort on my part. To have applied thought and effort to create what I wanted. To have taken the time. To have had the patience.

Life is like that too. The things that come easily to us can bring quite a lot of enjoyment and satisfaction. But they often pale in comparison to the things for which we have had to work—the things that challenge us. The things that require our thought, our care, our patience, and our time.

The life lessons we are given are not always going to be easy to process. There is not always going to be a—*click, whoosh*. We may really have to work. Hard. But in the end, what we have gained is so much more satisfying.

Thin Skin

They say that the first set of holidays after you lose someone is always the most difficult. (I mean … *duh*). Last year, as far as Christmas went, we just wanted to get through it—quick and dirty. We were all bracing ourselves for our first Christmas without Dad (not to mention the anniversary of his passing), and my mother was in the full throes of chemotherapy. Good times.

My family and I keep trying to remember the details of it. It's all just a foggy haze—although I do remember that my sister-in-law, Karen, wore an elf suit to Christmas dinner because she said everyone needed some Christmas spirit, and that my sister-in-law, Alexis, called it, "A Very Cancer Christmas." (Sometimes if you don't laugh, you'll cry. I guess we've done our fair share of both.)

And now, here we are, rounding the corner on two years since Dad died and …

I won't hold you in suspense. It isn't any easier. Not really.

Along with this, I will tell you, things for me have been good … so good. The girls (now nine and twelve) are great. My mother is healthy. I have lost the fifteen pounds of grief-weight I gained last year. Work feels fulfilling. We have so much for which to be grateful … and we are. I am. So grateful.

Still …

For the past few weeks, I have felt on the edge. I am so quick to well up with sadness—over a song, over a memory. I miss him. I have also been feeling the grief of others—those who have lost loved ones this year—so heavily. I carry it all with me.

It's as if I have a thinner skin now—as if, at any moment, my thin skin threatens to spill my very essence all over the floor, revealing the most raw and unapologetic parts of me.

My skin is barely containing me.

The good news is this. This thin skin keeps all of the good stuff right at the surface, too. I am feeling everything with intensity. Joy and gratitude—these are aching to burst forth as well. Every emotion courses through me, filling me up until it has nowhere to go but to leak from my eyes.

This evening, I found myself sitting by a fire in my beautiful new home, reading a book and enjoying a glass of wine. My two most favorite little ladies sat beside me—one drawing, one reading. I suddenly felt overwhelmed.

This is too good, I thought to myself. *This is a perfect moment. How did I get so lucky?*

Lately, I have been having dreams about a young mother who lost her battle with ovarian cancer just a few weeks ago. I did not know her well—hardly at all, really. When I first met her, she had just begun her battle with stage 4 cancer, and was already terminal. Yet, she seemed more full of life than most. She glowed. It's the kind of perversely glaring contrast that sticks with you.

Honestly, I can't make much sense of the dreams, but I feel as though I am seeing her, repeatedly, for a reason. If I had to guess, I'd say she has come to remind me. To remind me that it is okay to feel it all.

Because I am here. I have the privilege of being here—in my thin skin—feeling it all.

The Seed

At the beginning, just after Dad left us, I made reference to a feeling within myself, a "breaking open." I did not use this metaphor in a positive context, because quite frankly, I didn't see it that way. I meant, *My life has broken me. I am broken.*

Now, with some perspective, I can see that yes, I am broken—but I am not irreparable. Wait, that's not true. Actually, I *am* irreparable, because I was never meant to be repaired.

I do not require fixing.

I cannot go back into the seed casing. I cannot curl back into who I once was—and I don't want to. I am forever changed. I hope to break open and to bloom again and again. No, I do not wish for more hardship and tragedy in order to further become. Actually, I believe it is equally the joys in life that have the ability to break us open. Even the simplest of things can expand us when we open ourselves up to them—waking up in the morning next to someone we truly love, witnessing a fiery sunrise, or letting the sound of our children's laughter spill over us.

When we practice opening our hearts within these beautiful and simple moments, it is easier to begin to open them during our painful experiences as well. We can choose to soften when we feel the impulse to tighten. In opening our hearts to fully feel it all—the full spectrum of our humanity—we begin to trust in the courage of the seed.

Knowing that the moment we let go is when the light bursts through—as Mark Nepo writes, *"An awakening beyond all imagining."*

Epilogue

Quietly and conspiratorially, we cobble together two sandwiches from what is left over at the tail end of our week-long vacation—a few slices of roast beef, a small wedge of brie, some lettuce and tomato that we pull from a leftover salad. I grab a beer, and Mom pours her Manhattan into a plastic keg cup.

We always say we are going to have dinner on the beach during our annual family vacation to Florida, but the logistics of it with so many of us are prohibitive, and practicality always wins out. Dinner at the condos (five of them at this point, housing thirty people!) and then drinks on the beach at sunset is the usual format.

But today, my mother and I found ourselves alone on the beach in the early evening, and we knew it was our time to finally have that dinner on the beach. "Let's do it tonight," she said somewhat rebelliously, knowing we would be a no-show at the planned family dinner happening in a half an hour.

We grin at each other as we head down to the beach with our dinners balanced on paper plates. Toes in the sand, eyes out over the Gulf of Mexico, we agree that these are, in fact, the best sandwiches we've ever had. And the best beer. And the best Manhattan.

Last year when we took this trip, Mom was five weeks post-op from a double mastectomy. The year before that, we had just lost my dad. I can't explain how grateful I feel, sitting here with her, seeing her so happy and vibrant. So joyful.

A storm is approaching on the horizon, but still we hope to catch the sunset. And then the rain starts. Just a sprinkle.

"We have to go swimming!" she says. A declaration, not a question. This is a woman who often does not swim in the ocean even when it's a hot and sunny afternoon. How can I say no?

The ocean feels like a bathtub as the air around us grows cooler. The rain peppers our heads and makes percussion sounds and perfect ripples on the water's surface. I know I will remember this moment forever. Being here. With this survivor. This tender and fierce warrior that is my mother.

We hear thunder in the distance, and wonder aloud whether we should get out of the water, but the moment is too perfect.

Then … BOOM!

We shriek and laugh as we race out of the ocean and frantically gather our things from the beach. It begins to pour and crash around us as we run toward safety. Another crash. We toss our metal chairs somewhere along the way, agreeing we'll get them tomorrow.

"Your father is laughing right now!" she calls out to me through the rain.

"I have no doubt he is," I call back with a grin.

ACKNOWLEDGMENTS

To my loved ones: I hope you see and feel yourselves in these pages, whether or not you are called out by name. Thank you for your love, inspiration, and encouragement. This book would not exist without you. Especially you, dad.

Monica Rodgers, you believed in me and my writing from the very first sentence, and perhaps more passionately than anyone else. Thank you for never giving up on this book, and for knowing when to push me forward and when to give me the space to rise on my own.

Elizabeth Rose, thank you for your initial editing to prepare my first draft for my beta readers. Also, thanks to my beta readers, Tabitha, Mike, Jill, and Maureen, for taking the time to offer me your helpful and supportive feedback.

Bryna Haynes, my final editor and publisher—you are an absolute force of positivity and will. It has been a gift to work with you.

ABOUT THE AUTHOR

Bethany Harvey lives in Rhode Island with her two wise and wonderful daughters, two cats, and a Labrador who is blessed with an insatiable appetite and a wildly indiscriminate palate. She is the owner of Bloom, a highly sought-after, nature inspired preschool and childcare center.

The woods are her sanctuary, and adventuring on a paddle board is a close second. Her family is big and beautiful and an endless source of love, comfort, and laughter.

Bethany always enjoyed writing, but it wasn't until her life seemed to lay before her in ruins that she dedicated herself to using this passionate gift to express herself fully, and to invite others to feel it all with her.

Having been dubbed "Sunshine" as a child, Bethany always thought her gift to the world was in maintaining a sunny disposition, no matter what. However, she has come to know that grief and gratitude are not mutually exclusive. We are not less grateful in our depth and breadth of emotion—even (or especially) when we are called to sit with the dark ones awhile. Dipped In It was born through with the recognition that allowing ourselves to feel the full spectrum of human emotion (even the uncomfortable parts) is what keeps us alive and connected as human beings.

Learn more about Bethany and her work at www.DippedInIt. com.

ABOUT THE PUBLISHER

Founded in 2021 by Bryna Haynes, WorldChangers Media is a boutique publishing company focused on "Ideas for Impact."

We know that great books can change lives, topple outdated paradigms, and build movements. Our commitment is to deliver superior-quality transformational nonfiction by, and for, the next generation of thought leaders, conscious entrepreneurs, creatives, healers, and industry disruptors.

Ready to write and publish your thought leadership book with us? Learn more at www.WorldChangers.Media.

CPSIA information can be obtained
at www.ICGtesting.com
Printed in the USA
JSHW041425260822
29720JS00003B/12